Praise for *The Communication Code*

"In all of my years of leading organizations, positive relationships were the key tenants. If people can trust each other, then they can communicate effectively. The world needs better leaders, and *The Communication Code* gives you a set of tools to build better relationships to work together to enable cultures to serve the greater good with an integrated life, which is our love made visible."

—Alan Mulally, Former President and CEO of Boeing Commercial Airplanes and the Ford Motor Company

"I write songs to unlock people and get them to relax. Jeremie and Steve write books to do the same. This one is changing the way I deal with people. Don't miss it."

—Breland, Platinum Selling Recording Artist

"Who doesn't want to "unlock" every relationship in their life? This book is timely in this era of disconnection. Read it and win!"

—Molly Fletcher, author of *The Energy Clock* and host of the *Game Changers with Molly Fletcher* podcast

"Relationships are stories—some good, some bad. Jeremie and Steve have created a formula to reset what everyone wants—better relationships. Enjoy!"

—Nancy Duarte, CEO of Duarte and best-selling author

"Every single week I help people work on their relationships, and *The Communication Code* is one of my go-to tools that I use to help unlock people. I use it personally as well as in so many of my own relationships and can honestly say that if you use *The Communication Code,* you will drastically improve your life, almost immediately."

—Dr. Ed Newton, Sr. Pastor, CBC San Antonio

"I've been working with GiANT for years and can honestly say these tools work. *The Communication Code* is a mirror that challenges you to improve every relationship if you choose to accept it. You simply need to adopt it."

—Robert Kellogg, CEO, WatersEdge

"People need people, and when relationships don't work, nothing does. Really soak in this wisdom here as you attempt to reset the relationships that are most dear to you!"

—Bob Goff, author of *Love Does*

THE COMMUNICATION CODE

JEREMIE KUBICEK & STEVE COCKRAM

THE COMMUNICATION CODE

Unlock Every Relationship,
One Conversation At A Time

WILEY

Published by John Wiley & Sons, Inc., Hoboken, New Jersey.
Published simultaneously in Canada.

For general information on our other products and services or for technical support, please contact our Customer Care Department within the United States at (800) 762-2974, outside the United States at (317) 572-3993 or fax (317) 572-4002.

Wiley also publishes its books in a variety of electronic formats. Some content that appears in print may not be available in electronic formats. For more information about Wiley products, visit our web site at www.wiley.com.

Library of Congress Cataloging-in-Publication Data:

Names: Kubicek, Jeremie, author. | Cockram, Steve, author.
Title: The communication code : unlock every relationship, one conversation at a time / Jeremie Kubicek and Steve Cockram.
Description: Hoboken, New Jersey : Wiley, [2024] | Includes index.
Identifiers: LCCN 2023035111 (print) | LCCN 2023035112 (ebook) | ISBN 9781394150533 (cloth) | ISBN 9781394150557 (adobe pdf) | ISBN 9781394150540 (epub)
Subjects: LCSH: Interpersonal communication. | Communication in management.
Classification: LCC BF637.C45 K83 2024 (print) | LCC BF637.C45 (ebook) | DDC 153.6—dc23/eng/20230823
LC record available at https://lccn.loc.gov/2023035111
LC ebook record available at https://lccn.loc.gov/2023035112

Cover Design and Illustration: 99 Designs

SKY10055490_091523

Jeremie and Steve dedicate this book to those longing for a breakthrough in communicating with others. We hope you are inspired by this content and use it to transform your relationships for everyone's benefit.

Contents

Acknowledgments

We want to thank the incredible GiANT HQ team for the work it continues to do to serve leaders around the globe. Each of you bring so much to the table. Special thanks to Bronson Taylor and the leadership team for your consistency.

To the over one thousand Partners, Guides, and Catalysts, we are grateful for your partnership to raise up liberators and unlock the potential of people around the globe. What a privilege to link arms with you to do something bigger than we could do separately.

From Jeremie:

Kelly, thank you for believing in me every single day. I couldn't do it without you. I love you.

Addison, Will, and Kate, you are rock stars! I am so excited to see your influence and the companies you will lead. I am super proud of who you are and what you are doing to help so many.

Steve, we made it to 10 years. Let's go for another 10! Thanks for being there for me and pushing me to be the best version of myself.

Thanks also to Bryan Evans for allowing me a retreat location to write. It is always easier to write inspired. I am also grateful for my YPO forum—you are all amazing.

Special thanks to these partners for allowing me to be me on the projects we are working together on—Bronson Taylor, Kevin DeShazo, Will Kubicek, Tracy Rader, Clare Smith, and Mike Oppedahl. I respect you all!

Thanks for managing my world, Andrea Ediger and Anne O'Hea. You are so helpful.

Last, thanks to you, Mike and Kianna Kubicek, for being consistently supportive. I know you are for us. Words are not enough.

From Steve:

Helen, thank you for communicating with me so graciously every day for over 30 years—I have learned so much from you and my wonderful parents and in-laws, Ian and Sue Cockram, and Chris and Myra Adams.

Thank you to my three amazing daughters, Izzy, Megan, and Charlie, who keep me grounded and grateful.

Jeremie—what an adventure! It's not easy partnering with a pioneer. Sorry for all the critique I intended as collaboration, and thanks for teaching us to celebrate well.

To my local GiANT family, thank you for doing life with us and making it fun—Becky and Tim Barsellotti, Stu and Susie Wright, Jaz, Ed Ampaw-Farr, and Dan and Heather Joy. I should thank Maliks of Gerrards Cross for keeping us fed so well.

Finally, thanks to many lifelong friends who have deepened my understanding of how we communicate (and endured me talking about this during vacations)—Tracy and John Cotterell, Robert and Elspeth Hughes-Penney, Jonathan and Jenny Perry, Jon and Katherine Shaw, Terry and Jean O'Regan, John and Ash Marsh, and Rachel and Graham Hawley.

Introduction

Effective communication is the lifeblood of every healthy relationship.

So why does it have to be so complicated?

Healthy communication is one of the most challenging things to master. How often has someone shared information with you, and when they're finished, you respond with something that either offends them, disappoints them, or makes them mad?

Healthy communication is an exception, not the norm.

Having worked with leaders worldwide in every aspect of their lives, we've concluded that effective communication is the exception, not the norm. That's why so few relationships stay healthy over the long term.

It's as if someone you are in relationship with (at home or at work) had come to you expecting a specific response but didn't tell you what they really wanted. You then respond in your most natural way (according to your personality or your experiences) to what you thought they were asking. Instead of giving them the response they were hoping for, you miss it entirely by either trying to solve their problem, critiquing their approach, or even blowing it off, not realizing how important it was to them.

Intent is not enough—good people who care deeply about each other, who are trying to listen, still blow it.

The Communication Code helps solve that. It's a tool that can unlock relationships one conversation at a time by allowing you to set up communication to create a win-win for both parties. As a result, there is a successful connection. Using five simple cipher code words, you can verbally reach people with what they are expecting from you. The five code words are: *care*, *celebration*, *clarification*, *collaboration*, and *critique*.

By asking them what they want, they are giving you a clue to crack their code and help them. If you do this well, both people walk away feeling satisfied.

You are about to explore the depths of relationships and how to unlock your communication and build relational trust. This level of transformation in relationships is a gift. We want to help you obtain the tools and the process to rebuild past relationships and create healthy relationships from the start.

Everything you are about to read has been experienced directly between us. This entire concept and Communication Code tool were created out of our frustration with each other.

Over the past decade, this tool has been used inside teams in the world's largest organizations and everyday families. It is a concept, process, and system that unlocks people and helps them come alive in ways they never thought possible.

As for the two of us, we have become adept at mining out our areas of weakness, and communication is at the top. Our science is creating visual tools that make a common language that creates objectivity, not subjectivity, to help heal or solve some of the biggest problems in your life. Our design philosophy with all of our tools is that they are like mirrors that allow people to see themselves clearly and make the changes needed to grow.

Solving Relationships

This book is ultimately about relationships and how to establish or re-establish relational trust between two people.

Relationships (and people development) are often called *soft skills*. The truth is that they are the hardest skills to learn because there are so many dynamics affecting two people. Examples between two people include:

- The levels of security or immaturity
- Maturity or immaturity
- Personality dynamics
- Present orientation or future orientation
- Current levels of stress
- Levels of responsibility
- Past relational dynamics
- Other people are infringing on the relationship, and so on.

Our goal is that, by reading this book, you could take a problematic relationship and make it better, whether at home, at work, or both.

We want to help you take your relationships to the next level.

Becoming a People Whisperer

Have you ever met someone who just *got* you? They were easy to be with. You couldn't wait to reconnect because they seemed to care when you needed it, celebrate well, or clarify before critiquing your thoughts.

Effective communication comes more naturally to some; for most, it's a challenge and a skill set that must be learned. We have found a way to codify the principles of effective communication and then train others on how to use them, which is precisely why this book was written!

Suppose you have followed any of our past writings, specifically *The 5 Voices* and *The 5 Gears*. In that case, you will know that we create tools that are simple enough for a 13-year-old to learn the concepts, and tools to scale throughout families, teams, and organizations. The same is true with *The Communication Code*—it is designed for you to learn it and immediately apply it, and even better, teach it to others.

The goal is that you might not only solve a relationship issue, but also begin to master communication and learn how to be a people whisperer as you grow.

The Platinum Rule

Most people unknowingly misuse the Golden Rule of "Do unto others as you would have them do unto you."

The problem is that a large majority misapplies this rule by saying things like, "I don't need a hug, why should you?" or "I don't need to celebrate, why should you?" and so on.

The Platinum Rule, written by Dr. Tony Alessandra, encourages us to "Do unto others as they would want to be done to them." It is a subtle shift but pulls out the Golden Rule's best.

To improve your relationship, you must shift what you want and become more adept at understanding the other person's needs.

Unlocking Every Relationship

"Unlocking a relationship" refers to making significant and transformative changes to the dynamics, structure, or nature of a relationship—whether at home or at work. It involves implementing innovative and groundbreaking approaches to reshape the way individuals interact, communicate, and relate to each other within the relationship and within each conversation.

To unlock a relationship means to move beyond traditional patterns and expectations and to explore new possibilities for growth, connection, and fulfillment. It often entails challenging existing assumptions, dismantling unhealthy or unproductive behaviors, and embracing novel ways of thinking and relating.

This intentional focus requires a willingness to step out of comfort zones, challenge old patterns, and embrace change. It involves a shared commitment from both individuals to embark on a transformative journey together, seeking to create a relationship that is more fulfilling, authentic, and aligned with their evolving needs and values.

Increase Hope. Lighten the Load.

Transforming relationships is heavy lifting. It requires you to develop a conscious competence to restore trust and communicate to the next level. The tools we provide are designed to lighten your load and make building relationships more sustainable.

We are going to provide you with a visualization process you can practice in real time with every relationship in your life. As you enhance your relationships, you will build confidence, which will appear in other areas of your life.

By the end of this book, we want you to have a game plan to improve every meaningful relationship in your life and train you on how to improve every conversation you have on a daily basis. Feel free to mark up the book, highlight specific areas, or listen via audiobook and take notes as you go.

We can't wait to hear the stories of true relational transformation as you improve your communication and solve the issues that have been keeping you from true freedom.

We are pulling for you on this journey.

—Jeremie and Steve

1 The Secret of Relational Codes

People are enigmas. They are mysterious, puzzling, and sometimes challenging to understand. Knowing their thoughts or motives for doing certain things is typically quite tricky.

Everyone has a complex Communication Code that needs to be unlocked if trust is to be established in a relationship and if communication is to flow freely. Most people are blissfully unaware of this fact; consequently, they don't know how to help you connect with them.

"People are an enigma, wrapped in a mystery, shrouded in riddles, and coated in layers of complexity."
—Anand Nav

The enigma is found in the complexity of how to fully know someone—to be allowed in at the deepest levels of their life.

You are just as puzzling as anyone else. Just as you don't understand them, people in your life may not fully understand you either, nor how you operate, which makes the game of relationships tiring, frustrating, and thrilling at the same time.

In this chapter you will learn what communication is, how people engage in relationship-centric communication, and how to establish the trust needed to unlock others.

Complexity Is Complex

The complexity of our communication exists due to the nature of our personality, our nurtured upbringing, and the expectations of others. Add that the choices we have made affecting our outcomes mean that every human being, like a snowflake, is truly unique.

Our life experiences (nurture) lead us to make particular choices. When life hurts or disappoints us, we add another layer of complexity to our code, making it harder for people to connect with us because they don't know how to read us.

Over time, the Communication Code inside relationships can become impenetrable, and communication can become impossible, which might cause someone to pull away and think, "It isn't worth getting that close to them."

When people pull away, the result can create an unease in relationships and loneliness can set in. Loneliness is the despair of our age. We have never been more connected digitally yet more isolated relationally.

We have a way to change that!

Understanding Communication

Transmission of information is not communication. You can send a message repeatedly, but if the recipient doesn't understand the transmission, decode it properly, and confirm they have received it, then your message is only a one-way transmission.

Effective communication happens when the person receiving our transmission is aware of our expectations and intent, and can respond appropriately.

Communication, then, is the transmission of expectation or intent during this exchange. It involves a Sender + a Message + a Recipient, just like one satellite sends a message and another receives it.

Communication is the transmission and receiving of expectation or intent.

Communication between two parties aims to ensure that we are on the same page, relationally and transactionally. The better the relationship, the more transparent the communication. Conversely, the lower the relational trust, the less effective the communication. Repeated frustrations in trying to communicate eventually lead us to stop trying.

If you want better communication, you must understand how to unlock others and communicate your intent and expectations.

Missed Communication

Two co-workers, Ian and Jane, worked in the same department of a large corporation. Ian was responsible for collecting and analyzing data, while Jane created reports based on that data.

Ian was a very intelligent person, but he was not very good at communicating with others. He often sent Jane his reports without context or explanation, assuming she would understand everything independently.

Jane was different. She was an amiable and outgoing person who loved collaborating. However, she found it challenging to work with Ian because of his lack of communication. She would often have to spend hours trying to decipher his reports and would sometimes make incorrect assumptions, which would lead to errors in her work.

Despite Jane's attempts to share her frustrations with Ian, he never seemed to understand the problem. He continued to transmit his thoughts through long emails without any context or explanation, and their working relationship continued to suffer.

Over time, the tension between Ian and Jane grew, and they began to avoid each other whenever possible. This affected their work and the team's morale, and other colleagues noticed the strain between them.

Their manager noticed the problem and tried intervening, but Ian resisted. He felt that his reports were clear and concise, and he did not see the need to provide any additional explanation.

As time passed, Jane became increasingly frustrated with the situation. She started to dread receiving reports from Ian, knowing she would have to spend hours deciphering them. She tried to find ways to work around Ian, but it wasn't easy because their work was interconnected.

Unfortunately, their relationship never improved. Despite attempts by their manager to mediate, Ian remained stubborn and unwilling to change. Jane eventually left the company, unable to work in an environment where effective communication was not valued.

Two smart people needed help understanding the fundamental reality that the transmission of information is not communication. It takes two people to receive the intent and confirm their understanding.

Why People Create Codes

People create codes to protect themselves because relationships can be emotionally intense, and individuals may feel vulnerable or exposed inside these relationships.

Our relational codes can change over time as we experience life. When we are hurt, we add a new level of complexity to the code to avoid experiencing that pain again. This avoidance explains why people growing up in safe and healthy families have more straightforward relational codes to crack. Conversely, abuse, trauma, heartbreak, and loss can cause humans to add complexity to their relational code.

Self-awareness allows us to share our relational code clearly with others. It helps them understand how to connect more effectively.

Relational dynamics are complex, and the work has to start with each of us individually. What's it like to be on the other side of you in a relationship? What happens when you are accidental? How do you make it hard for people to relate and connect with you? The answers will differ for each of us, but it is important to understand.

For instance, I, Jeremie, am a Connector, Creative, Pioneer (ENFP in Myers Briggs). Steve is a Pioneer, Connector (ENTP in Myers Briggs). Human behavior is far more predictable than you would think, for us being able to share our Voice order communicates a considerable part of our relational code.

> GiANT, the company we founded, has excellent tools and lenses to help you understand your personality better. If you're unfamiliar with it, we suggest you take the 5 Voices assessment (details are in the endnotes).[1]

Maintaining healthy and vibrant long-term relationships requires understanding the relational dynamics of those in your life, and to do that, well, you will need tools and lenses to properly understand others.

Because people are not self-aware enough to share their codes, people remain complex enigmas, even to those closest to them. Occasionally, they appear to crack the other person's code, and communication is healthy. Still, neither party knows why, so it's hard to repeat. Ultimately, communication in the relationship remains frustrating, expectations diminish over time, and people either settle for the status quo or move on and try again with someone else.

The Most Complex Codes

In World War II, Germany created the ultimate code machine, called Enigma. It was built to encrypt and keep their communications safe so others couldn't decipher their top-secret maneuvers—just like people do to protect themselves from other people.

This machine was an electromechanical cipher machine that used a series of rotors to encrypt and decrypt messages. It has a keyboard for inputting text like a typewriter and a lamp board displaying the ciphertext. Each letter typed on the keypad would be transformed into a different letter or symbol, which made cracking the code nearly impossible.

The Allies considered the Enigma machine to be unbreakable. However, a team of codebreakers led by Alan Turing at Bletchley Park in England broke the Enigma code through ingenuity, advanced technology, and luck.

One of the techniques Turing and his team used was developing a machine called the Bombe. This machine was used to determine the settings of the rotors on the Enigma machine by simulating the encryption process and looking for patterns in the cipher text. The movie *The Imitation Game* highlights the team's dramatic approach to cracking the Enigma code.

Turing and his team were able to break the Enigma code regularly, which provided valuable intelligence to the Allies. They were a significant factor in the outcome of World War II. They shortened the war by several years and saved countless lives.

So why the history lesson? Precisely because some of your most important relationships may feel like the Enigma machine.

How to Break Codes

Breaking codes does not mean breaking people! It means working together to truly understand each other.

To build healthy relationships, you will need to crack the code of the person you seek to communicate with in the same way that Turing and his team cracked the Enigma code.

Here are some classic responses that indicate you haven't cracked the code of a certain relationship:

"Why didn't you do what I asked?"
"Why is it so hard to understand what I'm saying?"
"Are you deliberately trying to annoy me?"
"I feel like you never listen!"
"Why would you respond like that?"

Our job is to help you become a relationship expert without having to go to school for it.

We can help you learn how to decipher people's expectations, and begin to read and understand them better than they know themselves.

Stage One: Self-Awareness—You have to understand your code. Self-awareness is the foundation of others' awareness. How complex is your Communication Code?

Stage Two: Awareness of Others—Awareness of relational dynamics allows you to become curious and empathetic as others seek to connect with you. How complex is their Communication Code, and what has shaped it? Something extraordinary happens when both parties, however different, are working at understanding the relational code of the other.

Communication won't be transformed overnight, but with renewed hope for the future, more grace is extended in the relationship. We create a virtuous cycle of improvement rather than a downward spiral of increasing despair, leading to stage three.

Stage Three: Understanding—We then learn to ask better questions when people transmit information. We take the time to try and understand their intent and expectations before responding.

Stage Four: Decoding—The person sending the transmission of information sends the cipher so that the person on the other end of the message doesn't have to guess the intent or expectation. The cipher translates the transmission so that communication is simple; both parties have an essential role to play.

Understanding a Spouse's Code

As we share stories from our experiences, we have changed people's names, but have tried to make them as relatable as possible. Have you seen or experienced this?

Mike and Sarah had been married for 10 years, but they struggled to connect lately. Mike was a team leader for an insurance company, and Sarah worked as a leader in a nonprofit.

Their life and their kid's schedules caused them to live hectic, chaotic lives. While they loved each other deeply, they noticed more frequent arguing occurring, and it felt like they were drifting apart.

Sarah was an introvert and struggled to express her emotions to others. She was a Guardian in our 5 Voices language and would often bottle up her feelings, leading to misunderstandings and frustrations. On the other hand, Mike was an extrovert—a Connector who loved to talk out loud about his emotions and feelings. He couldn't understand why Sarah had difficulty communicating with him.

One day, after a particularly heated argument, Mike met with his executive coach to discuss how to have a relational breakthrough. He knew that something had to change, but was surprised when it started with looking in the mirror at himself. Mike's "aha" was in that they were indeed opposites. As his coach explained his personality in-depth, Mike began to see how different they were. He went on to understand his tendency to talk aloud and how that could frustrate Sarah regularly (stage one).

This session caused him to want to understand Sarah more. He started paying closer attention to Sarah's body language, and the subtle signals she would give off when upset or frustrated.

Slowly but surely, Mike started to understand Sarah's relational code (stage two) and could see the walls she had built to protect herself. He realized that when Sarah was upset, she would often retreat into herself and become very quiet. He started to recognize that this was a sign that she needed time to process her emotions and that he needed to give her space.

Processing with his coach gave him an outlet that led to positive outcomes instead of the typical miscommunication and the fights that would come with that.

Because of that counsel, Mike began to use a different approach (stage three) to communicate with Sarah. Instead of bombarding her with questions or forcing her to talk about her emotions, he would begin with a simple statement such as "I can see that you're upset, and I'm here to listen whenever you're ready to talk." He showed by his words and actions that he cared for her. This approach allowed Sarah to feel heard and understood without feeling pressured or judged.

Over time, Sarah started to open up more to Mike. She realized he was genuinely trying to understand her. She felt more comfortable sharing her cipher with him, telling him she wanted him to ask clarifying questions (stage four). Mike, for his part, was happy to see that Sarah was opening up more, and he was grateful for the breakthrough that they had made.

As a result of this breakthrough, Mike and Sarah's relationship improved significantly. They were able to communicate more effectively, and they were able to work through their problems together. They still had disagreements, but they could now work constructively and respectfully. Their willingness to to unlock their Communication Code's ultimately saved their marriage. It brought them closer together than ever before.

Marriage can be difficult, especially if one or both parties give up. Choosing to understand is crucial to cracking codes. It is the desire to fight for the highest possible good of your spouse that helps unlock them.

Making Progress

Few people truly understand the complexity and diversity of human behavior. Most remain unconsciously incompetent, doing for others what they would most want to be done for them and then wondering why the relationship doesn't work. That was historically true for both of us.

Like the Enigma code, people's Communication Codes can be opened with enough knowledge, effort, and time. As we progress through the book, we will explore ways to unlock others and train you to communicate more effectively.

Relationships are like a puzzle. The problem is that you often need the picture on the box to understand what it is supposed to look like. This book serves as the picture you will need to solve relationships and crack the codes of others in your life, whether at home or at work.

Our goal is to provide the cipher tools you need to crack the Communication Code, break down any relational drama, and reap the benefits of healthy relationships in every area of your life. If you are prepared to do the hard yards, we will help you become a people whisperer so that you can be an influencer for good in the world.

Before getting to the cipher, we must deal with the past and decide if the person is worth investing in for a breakthrough.

Note

1. Take the 5 Voices assessment at www.5voices.com to understand your voice order.

2 The Power of the Past

If you want relationships to progress healthily in the future, you must deal with any issues from the past.

The past carries more weight than we fully understand. It becomes more prominent over time as memories loom large in the minds of those we might have negatively affected by past actions. Remember, people have long memories.

> *How people have experienced you in the past directly affects how people experience you in the present.*

Are you fully aware of how people have experienced you in the past? You might be dumbfounded about how your past negatives affect your relationships today.

Here are three historical challenges that must be addressed that affect communication and relational depth:

1. Relational Trust
2. Misaligned Expectations
3. Power Dynamics

These issues complicate relationships and make restoration more difficult. Until you understand and deal with these three historical issues, you will not be able to have a breakthrough in your current relationships and may experience the following:

- Trust issues: If a person has been hurt or betrayed by you in the past, they may struggle with trusting you now, leading to insecurities and doubts, which can strain your relationship.
- Communication struggles: How you communicate in relationships is often shaped by your past experiences. For example, suppose you grew up in a family where

conflict was avoided. In that case, you may struggle to communicate your feelings or resolve disputes in a current relationship.
- Emotional baggage: Past traumas, such as abuse or neglect, can leave emotional scars that affect relationships. Someone who has experienced trauma may struggle with feelings of unworthiness or have difficulty opening up emotionally to others.
- Comparisons: Comparing current relationships to others can create unrealistic expectations or cause us to overlook the positive qualities of the relationship with another.
- Negative patterns: If someone repeatedly experiences the same problems in their relationships, it may be a sign of unresolved issues from the past that will need to be addressed.

Once you become aware of how historical issues impact communication in the present, you can deal more intelligently with your relationships in the present.

This chapter will reveal the techniques we've developed to help you deal with the power of the past as you restore your relationships.

Let's start with relational trust.

1. Relational Trust

To trust means to rely on another person because you feel entirely safe. You believe the other person is for you and has no intent or desire to hurt you. Trust is foundational to relationships because it allows you to open up and be vulnerable with another person without needing to watch your back.

If you broke that trust with a person in the past, their current view of you would be suspicion or self-preservation—not allowing yourself to be hurt by you again.

Relational dynamics can be positive or negative based on the past interactions experienced by both parties. Positive relational dynamics lead to mutual respect, trust, and open communication. In contrast, negative relational dynamics lead to distance, mistrust, caution, and suspicion.

Understanding and managing relational dynamics can be achieved by being aware of one's emotions and past behavior. If it is negative, it must be dealt with to progress in the present.

Doing this well can lead to the development of a new healthy relationship.

Understanding Power

Influence is the ability to affect or change someone somehow. Influence is the power to change someone, for good or bad. If you influence someone, you can sway the person to act in a particular manner.

Growing up, parents tend to watch which kids influence you as it can lead to negative or positive peer pressure. The same is true with adults. A boss can have a negative or positive influence. The same applies to friends, neighbors, co-workers, and family members.

The more influence a person has over another person, the more damage (or positive impact) a person will have on another. It is precisely why it is crucial to understand your power over another person. Do you need to be more aware of your power?

If you are not self-aware, you may misread body language or signaling from the other person. You might then misinterpret the other person without knowing your actions produce today's coldness.

A simple yet profound way to review your relational dynamics with another person is to assess yourself through the mirror of the Support Challenge Matrix (Figure 2.1).

We built this tool to help people see what it was like to be on the other side of themselves. As you look at the tool, you will notice high support/low support and high challenge/low challenge.

- High support is when you equip and resource others in a work environment or are emotionally present and caring with someone relationally.
- Low support means they are not receiving what they need to do their jobs or don't feel like you are for them relationally.
- High challenge is when you hold people accountable to the goals that have been set by you or both of you.
- Low challenge is when no clear expectations or standards are met, and the other person needs to learn how to respond or act.

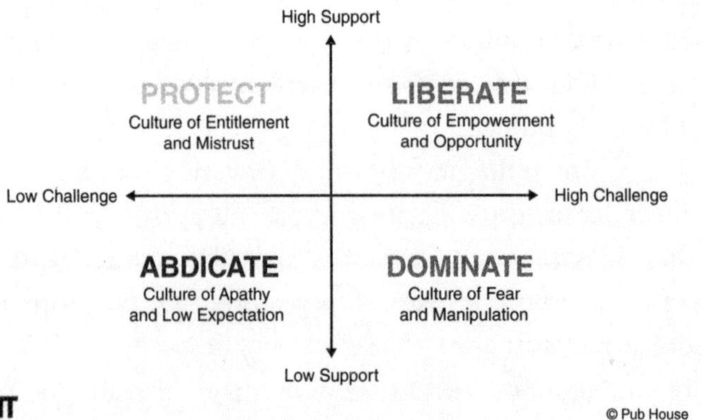

Figure 2.1 The Support Challenge Matrix.

The best leaders or relationships are those in the High support/High challenge quadrant.

These people provide enough support and then challenge the other person to be the best they can be. The results lead to a culture of empowerment and opportunity, producing trust and respect between two people.

Liberation Must Be Established

Suppose someone experiences dominating tendencies from another person. In that case, they will experience all challenge (typically through fear and manipulation) and little support. This style can lead to PTSD-like symptoms in a relationship and the walls of self-preservation rising to protect the person from the overbearing power of the other person.

Suppose someone experiences protecting tendencies of high support and no challenge. In that case, it usually leads to mistrust and entitlement as a person doesn't know the expectations, which is when enabling tends to occur.

Abdication is the lowest of all—low support/low challenge. The ramifications are apathy and low morale.

Liberation is when someone is free to be themselves because they experience High support and High challenge to be the best they can be.

To have a long-term impact on another person, you must establish High support before High challenge. It would help if you were consistent for some to experience you as a Liberating leader over time.

That means that if you are experiencing distance from someone, you will need to calibrate High support with High challenge over time for the other person to trust that you are really for them, not against them.

It is possible to address the issues from the past and rebuild trust in current relationships even after a significant breach.

However, doing so may take time, effort, and patience. It will require consistent liberating tendencies to show that one person is genuinely for the other.

Ultimately, the impact of the past on relational trust will depend on several factors, including the severity of past hurts, the individual's personality and coping style, and the quality of their current relationships. Both parties must work on stage one (self-awareness)—understanding how much the past has increased the complexity of the individual's Communication Code.

If you don't deal with the past appropriately, the past will continue to plague your relationship incessantly.

They can then help the person move to stage two (awareness of others), where they explore their past and code complexity levels.

Knowing these two foundational stages in relationship building will help people.

How Behavior Affects Behavior

John was a manager at a large company we had worked with for years. He had a reputation for being a strong and decisive leader, but he tended to dominate his subordinates and colleagues. He would often belittle or dismiss their ideas and opinions and demand that they follow his lead without question.

Lisa had worked with John for a few years. She was bright, talented, and had a strong work ethic, but she was often at odds with John's leadership style. John was notorious for interrupting Lisa during meetings, disregarding her suggestions, and micromanaging her work.

Over time, Lisa became frustrated and resentful of John's behavior. She found it hard to work with someone so domineering and dismissive. While she wanted the team and company to succeed, she needed to learn how to handle John.

Finally, Lisa approached John and expressed her concerns about his behavior. She explained how his domination was affecting her ability to work effectively. She asked if they could find a way to work together more collaboratively.

John listened to her concerns, became belligerent, and began to demean her in front of others. His behavior became so bad that his boss, whom we were helping, finally confronted him and told him to "change his ways."

John half-heartedly apologized, but his past actions wouldn't change his reputation. The team didn't believe it was genuine, as memories of his past behavior weren't resolved. He expressed his desire to be a better leader, but his behavior didn't change.

Why was John so unwilling to change? Why was John afraid of doing the self-awareness required to change the dynamics of his relationship with Lisa?

Lisa tried to help John, but he was ultimately unwilling or unable to hear the positive intent behind her challenge. Knowing the situation, Lisa was fighting for John's highest possible good, but he couldn't receive it from her.

Some historical trust issues in John existed that wouldn't allow him to receive from others.

While we didn't get a chance to work directly with John, we did discuss John's insecurities and domination with his boss to see if we could help solve the situation.

The damage from his past created damage in his present.

If John had truly apologized, he might have had a chance for redemption. However, John's behavior and leadership style would need to change over time to warrant a genuine belief that he was a leader worth following. Lisa eventually got promoted, and John was moved to a different division.

Ultimately, John was unresponsive, unprepared, and unable to engage with Lisa. When someone refuses to engage in stage one of their self-awareness, the other person can do nothing. Lisa tried to do stage two with John, but more was needed. (See Chapter 1 for a description of the four stages of relational self-awareness.)

Communication requires both parties to fully engage in making the breakthrough and cracking the relational codes. Lisa was willing. John was not.

This story is all too often experienced. The behavior of a leader affects the behavior of the team. The past can't be swept under the rug—it needs to be dealt with to build relational trust.

With that, think of one relationship in your life that you would like to improve and ask yourself, "What has it been like to be on the other side of me?" What would happen for you to be at peace with that person?

2. Managing Expectations

Rebuilding trust in a relationship can be challenging. You will need to reset expectations in order to reestablish the foundation of personal influence.

Expectations are ideas or beliefs about what will happen or what should happen in a specific situation or relationship. They are based on past experiences, as we have discussed, but also on the realities of today and the hopes for tomorrow.

William Shakespeare once wrote, "Expectation is the root of all heartache." While this may be true, it is virtually impossible not to have expectations of something or for someone.

Please learn how to have the proper expectations with another person. There is nothing more frustrating than two sets of expectations.

Conversely, when expectations are aligned, the chances of relational trust skyrockets.

Realistic Expectations

Realistic expectations are achievable and reasonable expectations, given the circumstances.

In the workplace, realistic expectations for an employee include meeting project deadlines, completing tasks accurately, and communicating effectively with others.

Unrealistic expectations might consist of expecting an employee to complete an entire project in an unreasonably short time or to work excessively long hours without rest.

In a personal relationship, realistic expectations include being respectful, supportive, and communicative with one another. In contrast, unrealistic expectations might consist of expecting a friend to meet all of one's emotional needs or to be perfect in every way.

Setting realistic expectations involves being honest and reasonable about what can be achieved and working collaboratively with others to establish achievable and beneficial expectations for everyone involved.

We created the Expectations Scale, shown in Figure 2.2, to help you visualize where you are in regard to your expectations with other people. Once you decide where you are on the scale then you must ask yourself whether or not you have clearly communicated those expectations with others. If not, then you could cause harm in the relationship without knowing it.

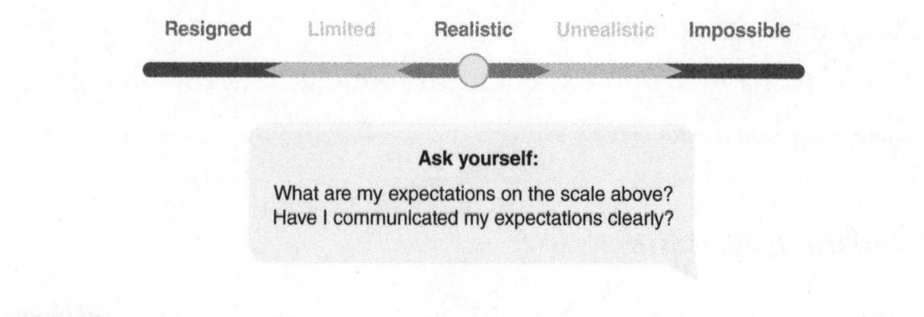

Figure 2.2 Expectations Scale.

Unrealistic Expectations

Unrealistic relational expectations are ones in a personal relationship that are unlikely to be met or are unreasonable, given the current realities. Unrealistic relational expectations can cause stress, frustration, and disappointment, ultimately damaging the relationship.

Some examples of unrealistic relational expectations might include

- Expecting the other person to read your mind: No one can read your mind, so it's unrealistic to expect someone always to know what you're thinking or feeling without communicating it to them.
- Expecting the other person to always agree with you: People have different opinions, and it's unrealistic to expect them to always agree with everything you say or do.
- Expecting someone to change who they are: It's unrealistic to expect another person to fundamentally change who they are or their values, beliefs, or personality traits because you expect them to.
- Expecting another person to be perfect: No one is perfect, and it's unrealistic to expect someone to be flawless.

Setting unrealistic relational expectations can strain a relationship unnecessarily and create unrealistic and unfair expectations for both parties. It's important to communicate openly and honestly with the other person and work collaboratively to set realistic and achievable expectations for both of you.

Checking Your Expectations

Chuck was in charge of a team of developers working on a software project. He was known for setting high expectations for his team members. Chuck was a hard worker and believed in delivering the best possible outcome. Still, he had a habit of setting unrealistic deadlines and goals.

At the beginning of the second quarter, Chuck assigned a new project to one of his team members, Todd. Chuck told Todd that the project was due in two weeks and needed to be perfect. Chuck had a habit of setting tight deadlines, but this one was particularly challenging.

Todd tried his best to complete the project on time but soon realized it was impossible to meet the deadline. Todd tried to explain to Chuck that the deadline was unrealistic and that he needed more time, but Chuck refused to listen. Chuck insisted that the project had to be completed on time, no matter what.

Todd worked late nights and weekends to try to complete the project. Still, he eventually reached a point where he had to acknowledge that he couldn't deliver what Chuck had expected. Todd felt frustrated, overwhelmed, and worried about the consequences of not meeting Chuck's expectations.

Finally, the deadline arrived, and Todd submitted the project, feeling exhausted and defeated. However, Chuck wanted more than the outcome. He criticized Todd for not meeting his expectations and blamed him for not working hard enough.

Todd felt demoralized and frustrated by Chuck's response. He thought that Chuck had set him up to fail by setting unrealistic expectations, and he worried about the impact on his reputation within the company.

Todd eventually realized he needed to speak up and set more realistic expectations with Chuck and other team members. He learned that it was essential to communicate clearly about timelines and goals and to push back when deadlines were not achievable. By doing so, Todd regained his confidence and trusted in his abilities. He eventually earned Chuck's respect by demonstrating his ability to deliver quality work on a realistic timeline.

This story reminds us that we all have expectations but must communicate them to ensure they are aligned.

Limited or Resigned Expectations

Resigned expectations are expectations that have been lowered or abandoned altogether due to a lack of hope or belief that they can be met. These expectations are often the result of repeated disappointment or failure to achieve desired outcomes.

For example, suppose someone has repeatedly applied for jobs and continues to experience rejection. This negativity may cause them to continue to lower their expectations to the point of resignation, which could cause them to lose hope and believe that they will never be able to find work in the future.

Similarly, in a personal relationship, someone may have resigned expectations if they have repeatedly tried to communicate with their partner and been met with defensiveness or avoidance. Eventually, they may stop trying to communicate altogether, believing their partner will never truly listen to them.

Resigned expectations can be harmful because they can lead to hopelessness and resignation, preventing individuals from acting or making positive changes. It's important to recognize when one's expectations have become resigned and to work to reframe them in a more positive and achievable way.

Alicia had worked at the same company for several years and was always a high performer.

She took pride in her work and always tried to go above and beyond what was expected of her. However, she needed help working with one of her colleagues, Stuart.

Stuart was known for being unreliable and disorganized. Alicia constantly had to clean up his messes and cover for his mistakes. She tried talking to him about the issues and offering suggestions to work better together, but Stuart was dismissive and defensive.

Alicia began to feel frustrated and exhausted from constantly picking up Stuart's slack. She started to lower her expectations of him and stopped trying to work collaboratively with him. She stopped offering suggestions and accepted that he would never change.

As a result, Alicia's work began to suffer. She stopped putting in the same level of effort and attention to detail as before, knowing that Stuart would likely mess things up anyway. She became resigned that her work with Stuart would always be a struggle, and she did the bare minimum to get by.

Unfortunately, Alicia's lowered expectations also affected her work with other colleagues. She found it difficult to trust and collaborate with others, assuming they would let her down. Over time, her performance suffered, and she became increasingly unhappy and unfulfilled in her job.

It wasn't until Alicia received feedback from her supervisor that she realized how much she had lowered her expectations and allowed Stuart's behavior to affect her work. She started to reframe her mindset and set more realistic and achievable expectations for herself and her colleagues. She also worked to develop better communication skills and to hold Stuart accountable for his mistakes rather than simply covering for him.

While it took time and effort, Alicia regained her confidence and improved her performance at work. She learned that it's essential to set high expectations for oneself and others, and be realistic and adaptable when faced with challenges.

When people's expectations are not met, it can lead to disappointment, frustration, or conflict. Expectations can also be a source of motivation and a way to set goals. In general, expectations are a set of beliefs that an individual holds about how things should be or will be.

"The quality of our expectations determines the quality of our action."—A. Godin.

3. Power Dynamics

Influence is power—the power to persuade others to do certain things. The intent of the person affects the outcome of the influence. Suppose the intent is for the highest good of others. In that case, the power will have positive results and lead to empowering actions. Conversely, if the intent is selfish or antagonistic, the outcomes will be adverse, leading to overpowering behaviors.

There are several ways in which people may attempt to overpower others, including:

- Physical force or intimidation: This can involve using physical strength or the threat of violence to exert power and control over another person.

- Verbal aggression: This can involve using hostile language, insults, or threats to intimidate or manipulate others.
- Emotional manipulation: This can involve using guilt, shame, or other emotional tactics to control the behavior of others.
- Withholding resources or opportunities: This can involve denying others access to resources such as money, education, or job opportunities to maintain power and control.
- Social pressure: This can involve using peer pressure, social norms, or other forms of social influence to manipulate or control the behavior of others.
- Know-it-allism: This can involve using one's experience or ability to control the behavior of others or to influence decision-making processes.

It's important to note that overpowering others can take many forms and occur in many different settings, including personal relationships, workplaces, and political contexts. By being aware of these dynamics, individuals can work to recognize and resist attempts at overpowering, and promote more equitable and respectful interactions with others.

Samantha was a new employee at a large company and was excited to be starting her first day on the job. However, as she walked into the office, she noticed a group of her co-workers huddled together, whispering and laughing. She couldn't help but feel a little uneasy.

As she settled into her workspace, one of her co-workers, Mark, approached her. Mark had a reputation for being a bit of a bully, and Samantha had heard rumors about his behavior from other colleagues.

"Hey, there," Mark said, his tone friendly but with a hint of something more sinister underneath. "Welcome to the team. I hope you're ready to work hard because we don't tolerate slackers around here."

Samantha felt her stomach knot up as she realized Mark was trying to intimidate her. She knew he was trying to establish dominance and assert his power over her, and she wasn't sure how to respond.

She took a deep breath and tried to remain calm. "Thank you for the welcome," she said, smiling. "I'm excited to be here and to work hard."

Mark leaned in a little closer, his tone turning more serious. "Good," he said. "Because if you don't, you'll be sorry."

He turned and walked away, leaving Samantha feeling shaken and uneasy. She knew she would have to be careful around Mark and be aware of his attempts to intimidate her.

Mark's unhealthy behavior showed up to Samantha and other co-workers like this:

- Controlling behavior: Mark tried to control their actions, decisions, or behavior in a way that felt manipulative or coercive.
- Blaming and criticism: He frequently criticized and blamed others for their problems or shortcomings and tried to make them feel guilty for their perceived lack of performance.
- Lack of boundaries: Mark disregarded limits and pushed his agenda onto team members without considering their feelings or desires.
- Dishonesty and deception: After watching Mark, he consistently deceived others using manipulation to take advantage.
- Disrespectful behavior: He displayed disrespectful behavior toward others, such as mocking, belittling, or insulting.
- Lack of empathy: Mark didn't show compassion or concern for their feelings or well-being and seemed to only care about his needs and desires.

- Self-centeredness: Mark was highly self-centered and prioritized his needs and desires above his team's without considering the impact overall.

Do you know someone that fits this description?

The Negative Power Test

We might all display traits similar to Marks, or at least parts of his behavior.

If you want to test yourself to see if you might be stifling your ability to improve your relationships, then assess yourself on the Negative Power Test. The goal here is not to bring judgment but rather awareness. If you see what it is like on the other side of you, you may desire to change for the benefit of all.

Think again of the one person you would like to improve a relationship with. As you ponder, ask yourself these questions to see how you score.

The Negative Power Test

A. Personality Power—As you relate to another person (choose a person in your mind), does your personality tend to: overpower, empower, or under-support this person?

B. Positional Power—Does your positional power (authority based on your role at work or home) tend to: overpower, empower, or under-support this person?

C. Personal Presence—Regarding your presence, do you tend to: overpower, empower or under-support this person?

D. Real Influence—Do you have a real, positive, imaginary, or zero influence in this person's life?

After answering these questions, we encourage you to ask the other person these hard but good questions:

How much trust do we have in our relationship?
How have you experienced me in terms of support/challenge?
How have we managed expectations in the past?
Where is our relationship on the expectations scale right now?

Asking these questions and going through the Negative Power Test starts a process of dealing maturely with past issues, and can positively impact your future and give you the best chance for relational breakthroughs.

In the next chapter, we'll learn the five code words to unlock the Communication Code of others.

3 The Communication Code

Relationships come in all shapes and sizes. Many are transactional, based on getting work done or accomplishing a specific task, while others are personal.

Communication changes based on the level of the relationship, whether shallow or deep. However, there is still a Communication Code that will unlock every person you meet with.

> *Effective communication is the master key that unlocks the door to true understanding and powerful connections.*

When two people meet, a specific expectation or agenda is usually tied to the meeting.

Typically, one person is setting the meeting, and it generally is that person that sets the agenda—at least in their mind. The other person may be clueless about what the other person is thinking or wanting. They may also be distracted from the meeting beforehand, or the extensive list of tasks might be overwhelming their minds.

The deeper the relationship, the deeper the expectation. Over time, if expectations are not met, bitterness will grow and undermine the relational dynamics between the two.

In this chapter we will give you the practical cipher of the five code words that can unlock a relationship and allow communication to flow.

Different Relationships. Different Codes.

Our lives are filled with many types of relationships. Some deep, some shallow. Old friendships and new acquaintances. Some are meaningful, while others are obligations—"have to" instead of "want to."

These different relationships have unique sets of codes to unlock. Examples of relationships and their differences include the dynamics of you and a/an:

- Spouse/partner
- Child/children
- Other family members
- Boss
- Co-worker
- Best friend
- Old friend
- Neighbor
- Team leader from another team, and so on.

We asked a friend how healthy their communication was based on the following list. Here are her results. You can take the same informal assessment to give you a basis for needed improvement.

How strong is your relationship with the following people (1–10; 10 being the highest)?

- Spouse/partner—7
- Child/children—8 & 9 (two kids)
- Family member—6 (Mom)
- Boss—5
- Co-worker—8 (Tammy)
- Best friend—9
- Old friend—7
- Neighbor—6.

How about you? Which relationship needs the most work and why?

Let's take that person and work on taking your communication to the next level. Begin by thinking through the historic relational dynamics to ensure nothing from the past will make communication impossible today.

It may be worth discussing the following questions:

- Are you both experiencing each other as liberators? (Use the Support Challenge Matrix in Chapter 2.)
- How would you describe the current level of expectation for healthy communication?
- Are there any power dynamics at play?

Remember, people are enigmas. In the same way as Alan Turing and his colleagues cracked the Enigma code, you too can change the relationship by understanding the codes of every relationship in your life. Suppose you're prepared to deal honestly with the historical issues and ensure the arteries are not blocked. In that case, we will give you the tools to take communication to a new level in every relationship.

A New Communication System

A Communication Code is a system of rules and expectations that connects two people or a group. It can take many forms, from easy nonverbal gestures to complex expectations.

We recommend a system in how you communicate, what you say to begin the conversation, and how you respond to others. We have found over the years that most relational issues occur because one or both parties are not intentional with their communication and the relationship itself.

If you want to improve the relationship, you must think ahead of what you want and learn the system in this chapter to improve. If you do it well, it will become natural to you over time.

Effective communication requires both the sender and receiver to understand the same language. That language must be objective, not subjective. Subjectivity can lead to a judgment that produces negative results.

The following story sets up the need for the Communication Code and how to do it.

Good to Bad

An infamous meeting occurred one spring evening just outside of London in the suburban village of Gerrards Cross. Two business partners (one British and one American) were meeting to catch up after the American partner returned from a significant trip to Atlanta for some significant meetings.

They met in a quaint and creative restaurant called Jack & Alice, whose atmosphere, food, and convenient location make it a favorite for many. They sat across one another in a booth by a window, wanting to talk more than eat.

Before the trip, they talked adamantly about the game plan, the hope of this specific meeting, and what it could mean to their young company. They listed what success would look like and role-played a bit about who would say what and how they could both win.

As the American entrepreneur started sharing excitement about the progress that had finally been made with a U.S.-based company, he couldn't get out the words fast enough, which didn't make it easy to follow. He had done this, talked to this contact, and held another critical conversation. He spoke enthusiastically and excitedly, but quickly saw that he might not be connecting.

It was true; his British business partner was getting lost, and without hesitation, said boldly, "So, wait, are you saying that we didn't do what we said we were going to do?" He then began to critique the returning partner with body language that expressed confusion and a smidge of frustration, saying, "I don't understand why you didn't do what we said."

The body language of the American shifted quickly from excitement to frustration as his eyes expressed a common frustration and then a steaming anger. The American firmly yelled, "Why can't you just celebrate?!" He went on a rant, saying things about the past, how hard it was to share, and how he wanted to celebrate without critique just once.

The atmosphere changed from celebration to frustration as the communication turned to miscommunication and unnecessary drama. Negative comments were made for 10–15 minutes as they tried to explain their feelings.

To their credit, these two business partners stayed in the conversation until they solved any issues. The next hour was spent analyzing their past meetings and sharing frustrations about how they talked.

They created a tool as they tended to do to help them solve their communication issue and ensure that it never happened again. When Jeremie Kubicek (the American business partner) and Steve Cockram (the British business partner) finished, they created a tool that organizations, families, and leaders worldwide have used. They made the Communication Code—a visual tool that can be used to solve problems and ensure that each person is heard and valued.

Turning Bad into Good

As we sat across from each other perplexed that our excitement had turned to frustration, it became clear that we didn't know what the other side truly wanted.

After returning from my trip, it was apparent that I wanted to celebrate but didn't think about what it might be like on the other side of me. I, therefore, overwhelmed Steve with random facts and connections while mentioning a partial deal I had negotiated that was not exactly what we had discussed but was the start of what could have been something big.

I could have better understood the logic of my business partner and how hard it was to follow me. Even more, I tended to be very defensive about critiquing at that stage of our business life, which wasn't easy on a logic-based thinker like Steve.

To make matters worse, I was reacting to Steve. I had pent-up frustrations from the past. I experienced Steve as a "no first" personality and prone to critique quickly. That triggered my defensive nature, and before you knew it, our reunion turned into an epic blowout in the quaint ambiance of Jack & Alice, of all places.

I don't know what others were thinking, but we stole some oxygen in the room as we talked for hours and left our drama on the table.

Oh, and did I mention our business was (and is) dedicated to helping people know themselves to lead themselves? We help leaders become the healthiest versions of themselves, to become leaders worth others following.

The good news is that we know how to use and turn those experiences into gold. Almost every one of our 70+ tools is simply us packaging our screw-ups so that you won't replicate our mistakes, but instead learn from them. GiANT's Leadership Toolkit is a visual codification of our struggles to make our two marriages, families, and business partnership work! They were created to help everyday people improve relationships.

The Communication Code

Steve needed a code word, but I didn't provide one. I was rambling, which was more common in that season of my maturity. He was asking critiquing questions, which was also familiar to his personality. At that table, at Jack & Alice, we wrote down this exact tool that can change your world if you let it.

Steve had just visited Bletchley Park with his kids, which made the Enigma story fresh on his mind. We immediately used the concept of a cipher before the transmission to help us understand what had just happened. Now we get to give it to you. (See Figure 3.1.)

The code word is the clue to the other person's expectations—the response they are hoping for but may not have told you. The more self-aware you are and the more you practice the Communication Code, the more natural it will be for you to understand the other person.

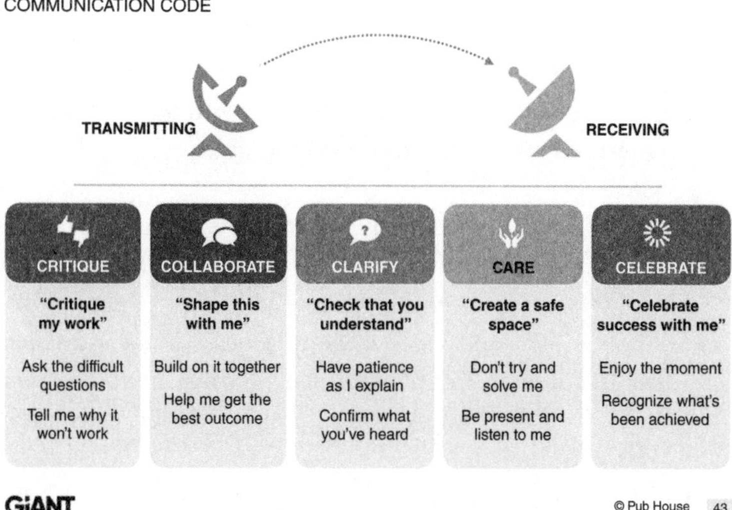

Figure 3.1 The Communication Code.

I wanted to *celebrate*, but Steve began to *critique*, thinking he was *collaborating*. The italicized words in the preceding sentence are the code words Steve and I needed to say and understand as such. By understanding the code words, we can use them effectively to unlock people naturally.

Let's break down each code word so we fully know what they mean.

Understanding the Code Words

It is important to learn the Communication Code words and train others in the language so that the objective words can help eliminate subjectivity that could create frustration and miscommunication.

Let's first learn the words and then we will share how to effectively use them to unlock the code in others.

- **Celebrate**

  To celebrate is to acknowledge (a significant or happy day or event) with a social gathering or enjoyable activity.

  When you share the code word: "I'm so encouraged, I'd love you to celebrate this success with me! Let's enjoy this moment and not move on too quickly."
- **Care**

  Care is being concerned for someone and desiring to do something for their good.

  When you share the code word: "I'm struggling right now—I just need a safe space to process aloud and share my frustrations. I don't need you to solve anything I say now; I need to know you're prepared to be truly present with me."
- **Clarify**

  Clarify means "to make (a statement or situation) less confusing and more clearly understandable."

When you share the code word: "I know I have something important to share; would you take the time to ask great questions so I can get it out? Please know that what I say first won't be where we end up, so be patient with me."

- **Collaborate**

  The definition of *collaborate* means "to work jointly on an activity, mainly to produce or create something."

  When you share the code word: "I'm inviting you to help shape this with me. I want your wisdom and expertise to help make sure we get the best possible outcome."

- **Critique**

  Critique is a somewhat formal word that typically refers to a careful judgment in which someone gives an opinion. It means to review or examine something critically.

  When you share the code word: "I'm inviting you to critique my work; I want you to ask the difficult questions! Do your due diligence—I need to know: why isn't this going to work?"

The idea here is that each person needs to understand what the other person is expecting—what it is that they want from you in that moment. Are you wanting celebration? If so, tell them that. Give them the code word so that they understand. Conversely, if you hear someone sharing something that may not make sense, clarify what you are hearing and ask them if it is okay to collaborate or ask them what code word they are wanting in that moment.

Doing this well will change the way people experience you. By using the Communication Code, you are setting each other up for clearer communication and eliminating the risk of misinterpretation.

Personality Tendencies

One of our GiANT guides shared a story of how personality affects communication: "One evening, my wife and I were in our bathroom getting ready for bed, and she said to me, 'You know, I know you often say you want to make sure everyone is taken care of in our family—and I can see that—but in our home, you're more of a doer, locking in on just getting things done.'

"I felt internally like that was 'a shot across the bow,' but I held it in. Instead, I used the Communication Code and asked, 'Is that a critique or celebration?' She said, 'It's a celebration! Nothing would get done here and be as organized without you pushing us along!'

"Whew! Crisis averted by what I took as offensive but wasn't!"

Using the Communication Code led to a deeper appreciation instead of an argument.

Clarifying ensures that relationships are aligned. How simple. Imagine your relationships when you begin to use this tool in your life.

If you understand your personality and wiring, you can understand your tendencies. In the same way, if you know the other person's personality, you can better predict their tendencies and relational code.

Years ago, we created the 5 Voices as a personality system to help people more easily understand each other. We broke down the natural tendencies of the present- and future-oriented thinkers and feelers. We showed how extroverts communicate versus introverts and so forth. The 5 Voices are pivotal to helping people understand others.[1]

Another person's personality clues you to their preference for their communication needs.

Communication is about being intentional, being mindful of historical issues, and listening well—thinking about where the other person is coming from and what they need most.

Knowing yourself can lead to better relational dynamics and becoming a people whisperer without people knowing what you are doing.

It works well personally or at work.

The Communication Code at Work

Consider implementing the Communication Code in your meetings to become more strategic at work. Here is a brilliant example of how:

Begin with Celebration.

It is natural for team leaders who are busy to start a meeting with their agenda items or begin to collaborate on areas to solve. This "collaboration" can quickly become a critique. If the other teammates have not felt any positive buildup historically, they may turn off from the start.

Instead, try celebrating for a few minutes to start the meeting. Here are some practical examples you can try within your team:

- "Let's begin with some celebration; what are some highlights over the past week/month?"
- "I want to start the meeting by celebrating Janice. Over the past month, she has hit her goals and is set up for another amazing month, and I want to high-five her for her diligence and hard work."

Celebration changes the relational dynamics of any meeting before getting down to the inevitable challenges. To celebrate is a form of support. We encourage you to make it genuine, or people will see it as flattery.

Here is another way an individual could use the Communication Code at work. Aaron Long, a consultant at GiANT, describes a client interaction. "I had a coaching client on a committee who was a Connector. He was frustrated with his team. He had some agenda items that were important to him for the organization. Still, critique would hijack his ideas when he would bring up the items in the committee meetings.

The organization had received training on GiANT tools, so I told him, "Next meeting, print off the Communication Code and take it with you. When it's your turn for the agenda, hold up the tool, point at it, and say, 'I need a chance to celebrate before we critique.""

The Communication Code at Home

Imagine building deeper relationships with your family using the Communication Code. What if you turned your dinner table into a communication lab?

Start with "What do you want to celebrate today?" Let that go as long as possible. It might be the topic for every day. Make sure to stay on the positive until a natural transition. Then ask, "Does anyone need any help on anything tonight?" This process shows care and allows someone to ask for help.

If there is anything off-topic, then clarify with something like this. "Are you asking if we. . . ." or "Do you mean. . . ." Getting this clarity will let you know what to do next.

If a moment arises to collaborate, ask permission with something like this. "Is it okay to collaborate right now?"

While celebration is a natural discipline for teams and family tables, the Communication Code works at its best when two people seek to connect 1:1. At home, that might be with a spouse or child where effective communication is needed.

The Communication Code is a tool to transform relationships by understanding the needs and expectations of the other person. It takes time to master it, but when you do, you will be amazed at how walls fall, and relationships begin to thrive.

The subsequent chapters go deeper into each of the categories. None of us are naturally good at all of them. We have Communication Codes that are default tendencies for us. Maturity is learning how to ask the right questions and respond in a way that meets the sender's expectations.

If you struggle in one particular area, then read and take notice as you practice mastering that area. Be sure also to teach the Communication Code to others. When you teach, you learn.

In the next few chapters, you will learn the depths of each code word and how to become proficient in communication and unlocking the codes of others.

Note

1. Take the 5 Voices assessment at www.5voices.com to understand your voice order.

4 Why Celebrating Works

"Celebration is a human need that will never go away. We need it now more than ever."
—Rita Moreno

Celebration is vital to the success of people and teams. It is desired and loathed simultaneously, a crucial part of the Communication Code. If you miss it, it can cause unnecessary drama.

Many people view celebrations as frivolous or not needed. They may believe that celebrations waste time and resources and detract from more important things. Employees can feel a lack of appreciation, which leads to team culture issues. We have seen this firsthand over the past decade.

The value of celebration can be misunderstood because it is often associated with external rewards, such as trophies or promotions. While these can be important, a celebration is not just about external recognition. It is also about recognizing and appreciating one's accomplishments and those of others and creating a sense of joy and fulfillment, which builds a solid cultural foundation.

A study published in the *Journal of Applied Psychology* found that teams celebrating their successes experience higher levels of job satisfaction, commitment, and shared identity among team members. The researchers suggest that celebrating successes helps reinforce positive behaviors and attitudes, increasing motivation and productivity. Additionally, celebrating successes can create community and teamwork, promoting a positive work environment.[1]

The need to celebrate is even more critical with the constant chaos that affects the majority of people in the world today. Yet, it rarely happens.

In this chapter, you will learn how to celebrate and why it is so vitally important to building trust and long-term influence.

Why Is Celebration So Hard?

So why don't people celebrate others more often?

Some people may have had negative experiences with celebration in the past. For example, they may have experienced disappointment or ridicule when trying to celebrate their achievements, which can lead to feelings of shame or embarrassment.

Alternatively, they may have experienced excessive or superficial celebrations, which can lead to disillusionment or disconnection.

Which one of these would you relate to?

- Being seen as insincere: Worrying that celebrating others will come across as fake, especially if they don't have a close relationship with the person they're celebrating.
- Fear of being perceived as favoritism: In some workplaces, celebrating one person's success over others can be seen as playing favorites or causing division among team members.
- Lack of awareness: Some people may need to be made aware of the importance of celebrating others or may need help understanding how to do it effectively.
- Cultural differences: Celebrating others can be viewed differently in different cultures. Some people may feel uncomfortable with certain types of celebrations.
- Personal insecurities: People who struggle with self-esteem or confidence may find it challenging to celebrate others because it highlights their own perceived shortcomings.

Celebrating others is a skill that can be learned and developed over time. By understanding the potential barriers to celebrating others and working to overcome them, people can become more comfortable celebrating others and create a more positive and supportive workplace culture.

Exaggerating Celebration

Have you ever been around someone who makes light of celebrating? They tend to exaggerate how distracting and annoying celebrations are. Why are people afraid of celebrating? Here are some areas we found. Do any of these fit you?

- Fear of unproductivity: Many leaders are afraid to celebrate others because if they do, the other person might not stay engaged or lose their desire to work hard. The opposite is true. This misconception about celebrating accomplishments frequently happens in sports, with coaches afraid to praise players so they don't become lazy.
- Fear of wasting time: People sometimes worry about others' view that celebration is frivolous or unnecessary and may see that person as wasting time on the company's dime.
- Not sure how people will respond: We have seen some leaders who are unsure how others will react to any celebrations and exaggerate how others would receive it, so they would rather play safe than mess it up.
- Long memories: Many leaders share past stories of when celebrations have gone wrong and use that as an excuse not to do anything at the moment. You hear things like, "Well, I remember one time we tried to throw a party, and several employees thought we were playing favorites. It messed everything up, so we should keep working and. . . ."
- Lack of understanding: Finally, some people may need help understanding the benefits of celebration or how to

> celebrate effectively. They roll their eyes at others doing it and think it is a waste of time. They need to understand the effectiveness of doing it correctly.

It may also be that you don't celebrate because you never learned how in your childhood.

When Celebration Has Never Been Valued

Did you grow up being able to celebrate? Not being able to celebrate is a real issue for many. A lot of people have yet to see celebration done well and therefore discount the power of it.

Mona is one such case. Mona's family was rigorous and conservative, and believed that celebrations were a waste of time and money. As a result, Mona could never celebrate her achievements or milestones.

Growing up, Mona felt like she was always missing out on the joys of life. She felt her hard work was never appreciated, and her accomplishments went unnoticed.

Mona continued to work hard and achieve great things. She excelled in school and was the top student in her class. Mona won awards and recognition for her achievements, but she wouldn't celebrate her achievements.

This lack of acknowledgment of her successes made Mona resentful and unhappy. Because she hadn't experienced celebration, she couldn't celebrate her success.

Mona's school held a ceremony at graduation to celebrate the graduating class's achievements. For the first time, she experienced the joy on her classmates' faces as they received their diplomas, and she realized the power of celebration. She realized that celebration was not just about marking achievements, but also about acknowledging hard work and creating memories.

After this, Mona celebrated her achievements in small ways. She would treat herself to a special meal or buy a small gift to mark the occasion. She also started to appreciate the little things in life, like spending time with friends and enjoying the beauty of nature.

Celebration was about marking achievements and creating joy, memories, and connections with others. Mona learned that even small celebrations could bring great happiness, and that life was too short not to enjoy it to the fullest.

Some View Celebration as Weakness

Is celebration a weakness? On the contrary, celebrating success and achievements can signify strength and confidence. Celebration is a way to acknowledge hard work, perseverance, and dedication and to recognize the progress made toward a goal. It can also help boost morale, motivation, and confidence, all critical qualities for success.

Some people may view celebration as a weakness because they associate it with excessive emotions or a lack of focus. However, celebration can be balanced and thoughtful, acknowledging success while focusing on future goals. It is vital to balance celebrating achievements and maintaining a drive to continue improving and reaching new heights.

Learning to balance celebration is an essential part of the Communication Code. If you view it as unnecessary, you will have difficulty connecting or relating to others, and most assuredly, not have the influence you desire.

When people celebrate their successes or the successes of others, it shows that they have a positive mindset and a growth-oriented perspective. Celebrating success can help people feel more motivated, engaged, and fulfilled in their work, leading to greater productivity and better outcomes for the organization.

Celebration is a vital tool for developing productive cultures.

Celebrating success is not a weakness, but a sign of a healthy individual.

How Different Personalities Celebrate

To use the Communication Code well, you must understand yourself from a personality perspective. Are you more of a thinker or a feeler?

Those with a thinking preference tend to be logical, rational, analytical, and impersonal in their decision-making. They ask challenging questions to get to the truth behind the data and enjoy the strategic challenge of aligning people, systems, and resources to deliver the most successful, profitable outcomes.

Those with a feeling preference tend to be compassionate, values-driven, and highly personal in their decision-making. They are highly empathetic and will work hard to preserve relational harmony whenever possible. They tend to be more sensitive to people's psychological state and can sense disturbances in the relational force that thinkers often miss.

Thinkers and feelers approach celebrating others differently.

Thinkers may focus more on achievements and accomplishments when celebrating others. In contrast, feelers may focus more on emotions and personal connections when celebrating others.

Thinkers may express their appreciation through logical and objective statements. Conversely, feelers may express gratitude through emotive and subjective language.

Thinkers may prefer to celebrate others in a more structured and organized way. In contrast, feelers may choose to honor others more spontaneously and informally.

Thinkers may focus more on the practical aspects of celebrating others, such as planning and executing the celebration. Feelers, on the other hand, may concentrate more on the emotional aspects, such as expressing genuine warmth and affection.

Thinkers may be more inclined to celebrate others privately, one-on-one, or in small groups. In contrast, feelers may be more willing to celebrate others publicly in front of a larger audience.

Everyone is unique and may approach celebrating others differently, regardless of their personality type. The most important thing is to be sincere and thoughtful in your celebration, and to find ways to make the other person feel genuinely appreciated and valued.

Know yourself so that you can celebrate in a way that is natural to you.

Start Meetings with Celebration

Celebration is an expression of gratitude. If you start with gratitude, your team meetings will become more effective. When others feel acknowledged for their hard work, they will be less prone to put up walls of self-preservation. Instead, they will lower their inhibitions and participate more effectively.

If, on the other hand, a team leader begins with critique, then others will be less prone to be honest, participate, or share helpful feedback because they have yet to experience that going well for anyone at any time in the past.

Leaders must establish the discipline of celebration to increase influence effectively. Every team faces complex challenges, and starting meetings with frustrations and challenges is tempting as you want to solve problems. However, beginning every meeting with the discipline of celebration changes the culture of team meetings. There are always achievements and people to celebrate; the challenges will eventually be addressed. Reminding everyone how the challenges and frustrations were overcome gives confidence that the team has the capacity and capability to do it again.

"Celebrate what you want to see more of." —Tom Peters

Celebrating others creates psychological safety, both for the person being honored and for the rest of the team, and it produces the following benefits:

- Increased happiness and positivity
- Strengthened relationships
- Improved self-esteem
- Reduced stress
- Increased motivation and productivity.

Jane had been working for the same company for five years. Still, when she started working for her current boss, Michael, she genuinely felt appreciated and valued.

Michael had a unique talent for celebrating the success of his employees, and he made a point to recognize even the most minor accomplishments.

One day, Jane completed a project that had taken her weeks. She was proud of her work, but wanted to know if anyone else would care. When she submitted the project to

Michael, he took the time to read through it thoroughly and then sent her an email congratulating her on a job well done. Later that week, he brought her a small gift and thanked her again for her hard work.

Michael didn't just celebrate the big wins, either. He was always quick to acknowledge when an employee had gone above and beyond, even if it was just completing a task ahead of schedule or coming up with a creative solution to a problem. He ensured everyone felt valued and appreciated, which showed in his team's positive attitude and high morale.

Because of Michael's leadership style, Jane felt motivated to work harder and do her best work. She knew her efforts wouldn't go unnoticed, and she felt confident in her abilities, knowing her boss believed in her. Over time, the team became more productive and engaged, and turnover rates decreased.

Michael's approach to celebrating the success of his employees had a ripple effect throughout the company, and he became known as a leader who truly cared about his team. His employees were more loyal, productive, and likely to stick around for the long haul—all because of his simple yet powerful way of celebrating their accomplishments.

When You Don't Celebrate

Conversely, not celebrating others at work can negatively impact the workplace and individuals. After assessing teams from over the past decade worldwide on GiANT's team performance assessment (Communication, Relationship, Alignment, Execution, and Capacity), the average score is 59%.

In our experience, an inability to celebrate highly correlates with poor team performance. Rather than creating more productivity, it produces:

- Decreased morale: When individuals are not recognized or celebrated for their accomplishments, it can decrease confidence. Employees may feel undervalued and unappreciated, leading to disengagement and reduced productivity.
- Lack of motivation: The absence of recognition or celebration can also lead to a lack of motivation. Employees may feel that their hard work could be noticed and are less likely to go above and beyond.
- Increased turnover: Employees who feel undervalued and unappreciated may start looking for opportunities elsewhere. Poor culture can lead to increased turnover, which can be costly for the company to recruit and train new employees.
- Negative workplace culture: The lack of celebration and recognition can contribute to a hostile workplace culture, where employees feel unsupported and undervalued, leading to a toxic work environment.

Not celebrating others at work has massive adverse side effects.

One of our GiANTs shares a story about a client that relates perfectly.

Anna had been working for the same company for three years and had always been a top performer. She consistently exceeded her goals and was known for her innovative ideas and hard work. However, Beth's new boss seemed to appreciate her efforts less than her previous boss.

Despite Anna's continued success, Beth rarely acknowledged or celebrated her accomplishments. When she submitted an awe-inspiring project, Beth responded with a quick "thanks" and moved on to the next task. Anna began to feel undervalued and unappreciated, and her motivation to work hard began to wane.

As time went on, Anna's performance began to suffer. She no longer had the same drive and enthusiasm she once had, and her work began to reflect that. Seeing that Anna's work wasn't up to her usual standards, Beth became frustrated and began criticizing her.

Anna, feeling unsupported and undervalued, eventually decided to leave the company. She found a job with a company that appreciated her contributions and celebrated her successes, and she was much happier there.

The ramifications of Beth's failure to celebrate Anna's accomplishments were significant. The company lost a valuable employee, and Beth's lack of appreciation and recognition contributed to a hostile workplace culture.

Other employees saw how Anna was treated and began to feel like their hard work wasn't valued, leading to decreased morale and increased turnover.

According to a survey by TINYpulse (an employee feedback platform), 79% of employees who quit their jobs cite a lack of appreciation as a key reason for leaving.

In contrast, companies that celebrate their employees' accomplishments tend to have higher retention rates, increased productivity, and a positive workplace culture. By recognizing and celebrating their employees' successes, leaders can create a supportive and motivating environment where everyone can thrive.

Why Celebration Wins

Celebrating the wins of others helps you win. If you are happy for them, they will be happy for you.

Dr. John Gottman has created a concept called the 5:1 Ratio Formula. Dr. Gottman's research suggests that there should be at least five positive comments or celebrations for every negative comment or criticism. Using the 5:1 Ratio, you can help create a culture of positivity and celebration, benefiting individuals and organizations.[2]

Celebrations create shared experiences. They show appreciation and recognition, which can strengthen bonds between people. Celebrations build culture by creating tradition.

Have we convinced you yet? Celebrations are vital to the success of your organizations, your families, and honestly, to you.

Heather had always been a hard-working and dedicated employee at her company. Still, she had never received much recognition for her efforts. She always felt that her work went unnoticed and unappreciated, taking a toll on her motivation and morale.

One day, her colleague David decided to take matters into his own hands and organized a surprise appreciation lunch for Heather. He asked his co-workers to write a simple affirmation on a 3×5 card and read it to her over lunch.

The surprise celebration completely took Heather aback. She was touched by the effort and thoughtfulness of her colleagues, and the outpouring of appreciation and recognition for her hard work.

From that day on, Heather's motivation and morale skyrocketed. She felt valued and appreciated, and her work performance improved significantly. She even started going above and beyond in her job, feeling inspired to give back to the team that had supported her.

David's simple act of celebrating Heather well had a profound impact on her life and career. It showed her that her work was valued and appreciated, inspiring her to be an even better employee and colleague. It also strengthened the bond between Heather and her colleagues, creating a sense of unity and camaraderie long after the celebration.

People win when you celebrate well. One small act of recognition and appreciation can have a ripple effect on someone's life and relationships.

Try This If You Don't Know What to Do

Celebrating another person is powerful but can be difficult for many. Here are some ways to honor someone, even if you are not that good at doing so:

- Start with gratitude: Recognize the contributions of others and express gratitude for their hard work. A simple "thank you" or writing a note of appreciation goes a long way.
- Write it down: When celebrating others, write down two to three things so they can reread them later. Be specific in your praise instead of sharing generic words.
- Make it personal: Celebrating others is about recognizing their unique talents and contributions. Take the time to get to know your colleagues and find ways to celebrate their successes in a way that is meaningful to them.
- Make it consistent: Celebrating others should be a regular part of the workplace culture, not just a one-time event. Please make a point to regularly recognize the achievements of your colleagues and make it a habit.
- Practice empathy: Put yourself in your colleague's shoes and consider how you want to be celebrated. What would

make you feel valued and appreciated? Use this as a guide for how to celebrate others.

- Ask for feedback: If you need help celebrating others effectively, ask for feedback from your colleagues. Ask them how they like to be recognized and what would make them feel appreciated.

Remember, celebrating others is essential to building positive relationships in the workplace, and creating a culture of support and appreciation.

What Happens When You Don't Take Time to Celebrate

Kim was a department team leader inside a large manufacturing company. She was highly respected for her expertise and professionalism. Still, she had a reputation for failing to be good at celebrating successes. Whenever her team achieved a significant milestone or completed a challenging project, Kim would acknowledge the achievement with only a quick email or a brief mention in a team meeting.

Her team was used to her management style and didn't expect a lot of celebration. However, over time, they began to feel demotivated and unappreciated. They worked long hours and faced numerous challenges to meet deadlines. They felt like their efforts needed to be recognized and appreciated.

Because of Kim's lack of celebration, the company culture began to suffer. The team members felt disconnected and needed more motivation, and their productivity declined. They felt like they were outside of a supportive and positive team culture, and many began looking for opportunities elsewhere.

> You will never create a genuinely liberating culture if you don't develop the discipline of celebration. Celebration is a type of High support that means so much to people. It represents a significant deposit in the relational trust account. It means they are better equipped to receive High challenge when needed. Now, back to the story.

As the team's performance continued to decline, the company's leadership began to take notice. The leaders realized the lack of celebration harmed the team's morale and productivity. They decided to bring in a consultant to help Kim and her team develop a more celebratory and joyous approach to leadership.

With the consultant's help, Kim understood the importance of celebrating successes and recognizing her team's achievements. She learned how to communicate her appreciation and recognition more meaningfully and positively. She started using the Communication Code to start her meetings with celebration, creating a more positive and engaging work environment.

Over time, the team's morale and productivity improved. The group felt more appreciated and valued and started working together more effectively. As a result, the company culture shifted toward a more positive and celebratory approach, and the team members felt more connected and engaged. This change also impacted Kim as she eventually moved to a higher position because of her team scores.

Employees who feel valued and appreciated for their hard work are more likely to be motivated, engaged, and committed to the company's success.

Celebrating Work without Affecting Work

If you are afraid that celebration will negatively impact work, here are some tips for celebrating work successes at work without causing disruption:

- Schedule celebrations outside of work hours: Consider scheduling celebrations outside of regular work hours, such as during lunch breaks or after work. This way, employees can participate in the celebration without impacting productivity.
- Keep celebrations brief: Keep celebrations short and sweet to minimize disruption to working. For example, a quick toast or a round of applause can go a long way in recognizing a work's success without taking up too much time.
- Plan celebrations in advance: Plan celebrations in advance to avoid last-minute disruptions to work.
- Keep celebrations low-key: Celebrations can be simple and inexpensive and still be meaningful. Consider simple gestures such as a thank-you note, a small gift, or a group email recognizing the work's success.
- Celebrate as a team: Celebrate work successes as a team to promote a sense of camaraderie and collaboration.

By doing these things, you can ensure the celebration is genuine and still retain productivity.

Monthly, Quarterly, Annually

A helpful way to ensure you are doing celebration well is to plan it. Make it a rhythm on your monthly, quarterly, and annual calendars.

Ask the Who, What, Where, and Why questions to help you organize it.

You can host a monthly team meeting by asking the following:

- Who needs to be there?
- What do we need to celebrate?
- Where do we want to meet?
- Why are we celebrating?

You can do the same with any quarterly meetings. We suggest making these off-site team retreats.

As for any annual celebration, make it memorable. Host an awards show or make it more meaningful by bringing spouses and providing unique gifts, typically around the holidays.

Little Big Things

When you celebrate the small things, well, big things will happen with your team or family.

Celebrations don't need to be extravagant and expensive. When you do the little things well, they make a huge difference. We call the following "little big things":

- Sending a random thank-you note.
- Giving a high-five to anyone for solid contributions.
- Celebrating the achievement of a co-worker's child.
- Posting a success of a colleague on social media.
- Calling or texting someone to thank them for something they did.

These are little things that create long-term goodwill. Others benefit, and so do you. You benefit on the inside as gratitude and improve your relational influence with others.

Employees regularly want to know that their skills and actions are valued. While small steps may not seem influential to the company's overall performance, they make a significant long-term difference.

Celebrating at Home

While busy at work, finding time to celebrate with your family can be challenging. "Little big things" applies at home as well. Here are some ideas to consider:

- Plan family outings: Small trips can make a big difference in the family dynamic.
- Write notes: One special handwritten note can impact your kids for years.
- Cook meals together: Create a rhythm on your family calendar to cook together.
- Create family traditions: Create two to three other traditions you will become known for outside the traditional holidays.

Remember, celebrating your family doesn't have to be a big production. Small gestures of appreciation and quality time spent together can go a long way in strengthening your family relationships.

Celebration Dinners

One of the hallmarks of GiANT is our celebration dinners. We have found ways to turn an average dinner into an affirmation experience. The concept is simple, but the execution is essential. An emcee typically leads these as you create a dinner (simple or fancy). Halfway through the meal, start the celebration with an emcee setting the rules.

The rules are simple: "Tonight, as you know, is a celebration dinner. I will give you the floor to celebrate another person in the room." The emcee may have asked one person to kick it off. Typically, it only takes a short time before the celebration begins, especially if there is goodwill between each other.

The celebration can last 15–20 minutes or four hours (true story). The key is creating an environment where it is okay to celebrate. A good emcee will make it feel natural without forcing the issue or going too long.

The results are life-changing as we have seen after hosting over 100 celebration dinners in our careers. A celebration dinner can happen at an annual event, a team retreat, or a family holiday. We have tried them in every type of environment. We have had "crusty old" men crying, those you thought would never shed a tear, share with others what would normally only be reserved for funeral speeches.

Why must appreciation only happen at funerals? You will be blown away by the outcomes when you share your feelings.

Here are some steps you can follow to throw a successful celebration dinner:

- Decide on the type of celebration dinner: Decide on the reason for the celebration, whether it's a team retreat, an annual awards night, a company or personal anniversary, graduation, or another special event.
- Choose the emcee: An emcee will make or break the celebration dinner. Pick one that others respect and can carry and hold a room. Try it for yourself, and it will make you a better facilitator.

- Choose whom you want to be there: Determine whom you want to invite to the celebration dinner, considering the size of your space and your budget.
- Pick a venue: Decide where to host the celebration dinner. It can be low-key or high-end. We have gone high-end and casual.
- Plan the menu: Choose a menu that is appropriate for the occasion, and that considers any dietary restrictions or preferences of your guests. You can either cook the meal yourself or hire a caterer.
- Decorate the space: Set the mood for the celebration dinner by decorating the room with appropriate decor and table settings.
- Invite the guests: Invite your guests with plenty of notice, and include details such as the date, time, location, and dress code.
- Prepare for the event: Set up the space and ensure everything is ready for your guests' arrival.
- Enjoy the celebration: Finally, enjoy the celebration dinner with your guests! Make sure to connect with each guest and make them feel welcome and appreciated.

Learn to Celebrate for Everyone's Benefit

You can celebrate a team when they hit a goal, receive great feedback, or complete a project. You can observe an individual for a promotion, hitting a quota, or delivering above and beyond. And you can celebrate your family for accomplishments at home or school.

Celebration is about being intentional. When you celebrate others, you become selfless and show that you can be present enough to see the value of others.

When you celebrate well, everyone wins.

In the next chapter, we will dive into how to really care. If you struggle with why you should care or how to do it, then that chapter is for you.

Notes

1. Grawitch, M. J., Ballard, D. W., & Marquardt, D. J. (2015). Accomplishment, accumulation, and activation of minor events: Differentiating affective influences of discrete work events. *Journal of Applied Psychology*, 100(6), 1718–1733. doi:10.1037/a0038554
2. The "5:1 Ratio Formula" was developed by Dr. John Gottman in *The Science of Trust: Emotional Attunement for Couples* (2011).

5 Why You Should Care

"The simple act of caring is heroic."
—Edward Albert

Caring is a misunderstood concept for many. Some invariably think that collaborating to improve things or solving presented problems is caring for the other person. These people, of which we are a part, have a harder time knowing how to care—it is our unconscious incompetence.

It's not like we don't care; it is more that we don't know how to care.

It gets even more difficult in the work environment when customers, bosses, and tasks can overwhelm the human trait of caring for other people. When a spouse calls with a need or a child reaches out, many often don't know how to show care when they feel work pressure. It becomes challenging to handle when a co-worker shares some pains, or you can tell an employee is dealing with a problem.

Care is being concerned for someone and desiring to do something for their good.

When someone shares their communication code word, such as: "I'm struggling right now—I just need a safe space to process out loud and share my frustrations," that is a request from them for others to show care.

People want to be cared for because it fulfills a basic human need for social connection, love, and support. We are social creatures who thrive on positive interactions with others, and feeling cared for is one way to fulfill this need. Others don't need you to solve anything; they need to know you're prepared to be with them.

Inside the Communication Code, care is fundamental. If you do not feel cared for, you will most likely not receive the transmission of the other person well. Your walls of self-preservation will increase, not decrease.

Care can be expressed in many different ways, from simple acts of kindness and consideration to more complex forms of support. Sometimes caring is an act of service that does solve a problem. Ultimately, care is about being present and attentive to the needs of others and taking action to help them feel safe, supported, and valued.

In this chapter, you will learn why care is important and how to do it well if you are not good at it. We both struggle with knowing how to care, so some of our experiences might be particularly helpful.

"I have learned that people will forget what you said, people will forget what you did, but people will never forget how you made them feel." —Maya Angelou

---

Care Is Shelter

Care, like shelter, provides security, protection, and comfort. Just as a physical shelter protects individuals from the elements and provides a safe space to rest and recover, care can provide emotional support, comfort, and a sense of safety in times of need to those in your life.

Just as a shelter requires upkeep and maintenance to remain effective, care also requires ongoing attention and effort. You can't give what you don't possess, and it is hard to sustain if you don't feel supported.

"To give and receive care is reassuring and validating; it creates a sense of shelter that touches the very core of our humanness." —Myra J. Martinez

---

Remember the last emotional storm you went through personally. Who was there for you? What did they do? When my (Jeremie) wife and I were in a near-tragic car accident in a hurricane in Mexico, I will never forget the care shown to us by some of our closest friends, my parents, and a few friends who covered us in various ways.

We were in a storm, yet those people's care communicated a profound love. We felt security amid insecurity and comfort when we were far from it.

Think about those whom you would call at 2 a.m. if you needed help—those are the ones whom you know genuinely care about you the most.

What People Need

Some might dismiss care and want to skip forward to other sections. Please take the time and understand what it is that people need. Here is what people want when they think of care:

- Emotional support: When people feel cared for, they feel emotionally supported. Knowing that someone cares about them and is there to listen and offer advice or comfort can be exceptionally comforting during difficult times.
- Security: Feeling cared for can also provide a sense of security. Knowing that someone has our back and is there to help us in need can make us feel safer and more secure.
- Affirmation: Being cared for is also a way of receiving validation from others. When someone cares for us, they affirm that we matter and that our feelings and needs are essential.
- Bonding: Being cared for also provides a sense of connection with others. When someone cares for us, we feel a bond with them, and this bond can help us feel more connected to our communities and society as a whole.

Being cared for is being loved and valued. It is interesting that while Care might be complicated for you, you may live or work with someone who deeply cares, and the best way to care for them is to care about what they care about.

Steve could see that Helen was upset and wasn't fully herself. Being a caring husband, he asked her what was happening and offered to help. Helen then gave several practical and relational scenarios contributing to her stress levels.

Steve, seeing how most of these issues could be solved, launched into full consulting mode, rolled out his large whiteboard from the office, and set it up in the living room. With colored whiteboard pens, Steve listed the issues Helen had presented and started to take each around the CORE process.

From his perspective, this would be a great date night and a chance to love Helen by using the superpowers others valued so highly. It didn't go well.

Helen was in tears and blurted, "You just don't get me, do you?" Steve, confused and frustrated, agreed. "You're right I don't get you, I'm doing my very best to help you solve the various issues you've raised, and now you're in tears. Are you aware I'm good at this? People pay me money to help them process their issues on my whiteboard."

At this stage in his life, there wasn't Communication Code language that he could use.

Helen wasn't asking to be solved. What she shared aloud were not the real issues. She was really asking Steve to care, to be present, listen, empathize, and give her quality time and simply be with her in her frustrations.

Steve defaulted to collaboration without relational cues or cipher, seeking to help solve the presenting issues. Expectations for effective communication dropped a level that night. If they were limited before, they were now heading to resigned. Neither fully understood why the other was responding the way they were.

When Did You Stop Being Cared For?

Those who have not been cared for in the past can often struggle to care for others well in the present. We have a well-known saying we like to use—you can't give what you don't possess.

Erik Erikson's Psychosocial Theory is a well-known and influential theory in developmental psychology that describes how individuals develop across their lifespan. He proposes that individuals go through eight distinct psychosocial stages, each characterized by a specific developmental task. The stages are:

1. Trust versus Mistrust (infancy): In the first stage, infants learn to develop a sense of trust or mistrust in their environment and caregivers/parents. This is based on whether their primary food, comfort, and security needs are consistently met.
2. Autonomy versus Shame and Doubt (toddlerhood): In the second stage, toddlers develop a sense of autonomy and independence as they explore their environment and assert their will. This stage is marked by the "terrible twos," as toddlers often push boundaries and test limits. Parents' responses to their child's attempts at independence can either support or undermine their sense of autonomy.
3. Initiative versus Guilt (preschool): In the third stage, preschoolers develop a sense of initiative as they take on new challenges and engage in imaginative play. However, they may also experience guilt if their efforts are met with criticism or disapproval.
4. Industry versus Inferiority (elementary school): Children develop a sense of industry in the fourth stage by taking on more complex tasks and engaging in formal education. Success in this stage can lead to feelings of competence and self-esteem. At the same time, failure can result in feelings of inferiority and inadequacy.

5. Identity versus Role Confusion (adolescence): In the fifth stage, adolescents navigate the complex process of forming an identity and developing a sense of self. This involves exploring different roles and values and deciding who they want to be in adulthood.
6. Intimacy versus Isolation (young adulthood): In the sixth stage, young adults form intimate relationships with others and develop a sense of closeness and connection. Failure to do so can lead to feelings of isolation and loneliness.
7. Generativity versus Stagnation (middle adulthood): In the seventh stage, middle-aged adults focus on contributing to society and leaving a positive legacy for future generations. Failure to do so can result in feelings of stagnation and unfulfillment.
8. Ego Integrity versus Despair (late adulthood): In the final stage, older adults reflect on their lives and come to terms with their mortality. Those who feel a sense of integrity and accomplishment can face death with acceptance. In contrast, those who feel a sense of despair or regret may struggle with the end of life.[1]

Erikson believed that social context plays a crucial role in shaping an individual's development. He argued that individuals are social beings shaped by their interactions with others, and that the social context can either facilitate or hinder their development, which would cause their ability to care to be limited to that era of life.

If at any point in time you didn't receive care, it could stunt your ability to give it to others.

Here is a summary of why this is important to understand the preceding realities.

- Learning to express care appropriately is required to be a liberating influence in someone's life.

- We often express care the same way we wish to receive it and get frustrated when that doesn't work.
- Learning to care appropriately takes time and intentionality. We have to learn how to unlock the relational code and win trust.
- Those who have experienced no, limited, or ill-directed care will struggle to do it effectively for others.
- Care is a skill that can be learned if we are willing to invest the time.

Upon writing this chapter, a text came in from a dear friend about the death of his adult daughter. This daughter had a tough life amid exceptional care from her family. I stopped writing and began to ponder what level of care my friend needed with what I could provide from thousands of miles away—prayer, comfort, a letter.

Caring for others is an art and a science. You can get better at it even if it is unnatural for you.

Is It the Reason You Don't Care?

Alex had a difficult childhood. Alex's parents were emotionally distant and often absent during infancy, leading to a lack of trust in caregivers and the world around him. In toddlerhood, Alex was left to his own devices, and felt ashamed and doubtful of his abilities. As a preschooler, he struggled to take the initiative. He was often met with punishment and criticism, leading to feelings of guilt and inadequacy. Throughout elementary school, Alex felt unsupported and struggled with feelings of inferiority.

As Alex entered adolescence, he became rebellious and sought validation from his peers. He struggled to form a strong identity and often felt lost and disconnected from others. Alex worked to develop intimate relationships in young adulthood and often felt isolated and alone.

He had difficulty providing care and support to others as his emotional needs were unmet.

As he entered middle age, he felt increasingly frustrated and unfulfilled. He struggled to find meaning and purpose in his life and often thought he had nothing to offer others. He began to resent those around him who seemed to have a more fulfilling and supportive upbringing.

Despite his harrowing experiences, Alex never sought help or support to resolve his issues.

He remained stuck in his negative patterns and struggled to provide care and support to those around him. His mistrust and fear of vulnerability made it challenging to connect with others, and he often felt resentful and bitter.

In the end, Alex never fully resolved his issues and struggled to provide care and support to others. He lived a life marked by a sense of unfulfillment and frustration, never fully able to break free from the negative patterns of his past.

While depressing, this story occurs time and again. The long-term reality is that because Alex didn't receive care and never resolved it, he cannot give care, which multiplies the issue until someone breaks the chain.

When people stop caring, it can negatively impact themselves, others around them, and their relationships. Not managing negatively affects society, leading to a lack of social cohesion, decreased trust, and increased social problems.

When people stop caring, the world becomes a much darker place.

We have the power to change this pattern. It starts with caring for the person on the other side of you.

Fighting Can Be Caring

There are many reasons why people should care for others. At GiANT, we have a phrasc that mimics a definition of *love*. Caring for someone means "Fight for the highest possible good in the life of those you lead."

We were inspired by the work of Kevin Weaver on this subject, and with permission, tailored it to fit our community. Caring means fighting. Often, caring is too soft of a word. It is tied to caregivers, nurses, teachers, moms, and so on. It is the task of looking out for and providing for the needs of others.

Caring is like a brother fighting for the best of a sibling. It is an honor, more than just an obligation. To help us to fight for the best of another person. We need more fighters, more people who care.

One of the saddest things in life is when two people who care deeply for each other begin to drift apart. This occurs because they begin lowering their expectations of each other and stop fighting for the highest possible good in each other. When this occurs, it is a clear sign of problems in the relationship.

We should care because it is what is best for others and helps us.

Allan Luks introduced an exciting reality in his book *The Healing Power of Doing Good*. The "helper's high" concept was coined after Luks conducted a study in which he surveyed 3,000 volunteers who engaged in various helping behaviors, such as caring for others directly and offering emotional support to friends or family members. He found that most respondents reported experiencing positive feelings, including a "helper's high," after engaging in these behaviors.

The "helper's high" describes the positive feelings individuals may experience after engaging in helping behaviors. It is often described as a feeling of warmth or euphoria. It is believed to be due to the release of endorphins and other mood-boosting chemicals in the brain.

When we care, we help others, and in the process, help ourselves.

How to Care Well

Caring well for someone else regarding communication involves several vital aspects. Here are some tips on how to communicate in a caring and supportive way:

1. Listen actively: Give the person your full attention and focus on what they say. Show that you are interested in their thoughts and feelings by maintaining eye contact and using verbal and nonverbal cues to show that you are engaged.
2. Show empathy: Try to put yourself in the other person's shoes and imagine how they might feel. Use phrases like "I understand" or "That sounds tough" to convey that you are there for them.
3. Validate their feelings: Acknowledge the other person's emotions and let them know they are valid. You can say things like, "I can see why you would feel that way," or "It's okay to be upset."
4. Avoid judgment: Avoid making assumptions or passing judgment on the other person. Instead, focus on understanding their perspective and providing support.
5. Be respectful: Treat the other person with respect and kindness. Avoid interrupting them, using a condescending tone, or dismissing their feelings.
6. Ask open-ended questions: This type of question encourages others to share their thoughts and feelings more. This can help them feel heard and understood.

7. Offer support: Let the other person know you are there for them and willing to help however you can. You can offer practical support like running errands, or emotional support like listening and offering encouragement.

You can learn to care, even if it is unnatural.

How to Care for an Employee

If you lead others, you can care for your employees by creating a work environment prioritizing their well-being, growth, and success. By prioritizing their needs and investing in their development, you can foster a culture of care and support that will benefit your employees and your organization.

Maslow's hierarchy of needs can be applied to the work environment to help understand the different needs of employees and how they can be met. Here's how the order can be adapted for the workplace:

Physiological needs: This hierarchy level includes basic needs such as food, water, shelter, and rest. This means providing a safe and comfortable work environment, adequate breaks and rest periods, and access to healthy food and water.

Safety needs: This level includes physical and emotional safety and security. This means providing a safe and secure work environment, clear guidelines and procedures, and support for employees experiencing harassment, discrimination, or other forms of mistreatment.

Social needs: This level includes social connection, belonging, and friendship. In the workplace, this translates to fostering a positive and inclusive work culture, providing opportunities for team building and collaboration, and encouraging employee social interactions.

Esteem needs: This level includes recognition, respect, and a sense of achievement. This translates to recognizing and rewarding employee accomplishments, providing professional growth and development opportunities, and creating a work culture that values and respects employees.

Self-actualization needs: This level includes personal growth, fulfillment, and self-actualization. This means providing employees opportunities to use their skills and talents in the workplace, encouraging creativity and innovation, and creating a work culture that supports personal and professional growth.

By understanding and addressing the different needs of employees at each level of Maslow's hierarchy, employers can create a work environment that supports their employees' well-being, growth, and success. This can lead to higher job satisfaction, increased productivity, and a positive work culture overall.

"If you take care of your employees, they will take care of your customers, and your business will take care of itself." —J. W. Marriott Jr., Executive Chairman of Marriott International

Years ago, I (Jeremie) spoke at an event at the famous Camelback Lodge in Scottsdale, Arizona. It was April, and the fragrance from the cactus blooms and the perfect weather made my dinner on the patio quite bearable.

I noticed a gentleman sitting alone next to me, and he breathed in and said, "Doesn't that smell amazing?" I nodded in agreement, and we struck up a conversation. He started telling me stories about the place and how amazing the people were. "I have been coming here for years and am amazed at the staff. They are just as amazing as the weather." That was interesting. We shook hands, and he said goodnight.

The waitress immediately approached me and asked me, "You know who that was? That was Bill Marriott—he owns the place!" She said the culture was terrific because they genuinely cared for the people. She continued by sharing how she was cared for numerous times when her kids were younger, which endeared her to the company. Bill Marriott then became a symbol of that type of care.

I was dumbfounded. The chairman of Marriott was enjoying a meal, and sharing how much he cared about the place and the people.

If you don't care, others will have a hard time caring.

Showing Care for Your Family

The same is true for your family. Our good friend, Louis Upkins, wrote a book called *Treat Me Like a Customer.*

In the book, Louis emphasizes the importance of treating everyone, including oneself, with respect, empathy, and a customer service mindset. He believes treating others as valued customers can build strong relationships, increase loyalty, and ultimately achieve success in all aspects of life.

Imagine treating your family like your best customer. That is the liberator mindset—the act of providing High support and High challenge. That might include the following list.

- Listen actively: When your partner speaks, give them your full attention, and show that you are listening by responding thoughtfully and asking questions.
- Show affection: Physical touches, like hugs and kisses, can help your partner feel loved and cared for.
- Support their goals: Encourage your partner's personal and professional growth by supporting their dreams and aspirations.

- Show appreciation: Take the time to acknowledge and appreciate what your partner does for you and your family.
- Spend quality time together: Make time for regular date nights or other activities you enjoy and use to connect and strengthen your relationship.
- Help out with household tasks: Take on some of the household chores to help ease your partner's workload and show that you are willing to help out.
- Express your feelings: Let your partner know how much you care for them and how much they mean to you. Verbalizing your feelings can help strengthen your bond and make your partner feel loved and appreciated.

Showing Care to Thinkers

To show care for a thinker, you can do the following:

- Listen actively: Pay attention to what the thinker is saying and give them your full attention. Show that you are interested in their ideas and thoughts.
- Validate their thoughts: Let the thinker know that their thoughts are important and that you value their opinions. Even if you do not agree with everything they say, acknowledge their perspective and show respect for their ideas.
- Encourage their curiosity: Thinkers are naturally curious and enjoy exploring new ideas. Encourage them to continue learning and growing by asking questions and engaging in meaningful conversations.
- Provide feedback: Offer constructive feedback that helps the thinker refine their ideas and perspectives. Avoid being critical or dismissive of their thoughts, but instead offer feedback that encourages them to explore their ideas further.

- Support their passions: Thinkers are often passionate about specific topics or areas of interest. Show support for their passions by encouraging them to pursue their interests, sharing relevant resources or materials, or even joining them in their pursuits.

The key to showing care for a thinker is to be present, respectful, and supportive of their ideas and passions.

Showing Care to Feelers

To show care for a feeler, you can do the following:

- Listen with empathy: Feelers are more sensitive to emotions and feelings than thinkers. Show that you care by listening to their concerns and feelings without judgment. Try to put yourself in their shoes and understand their origins.
- Show affection: Feelers often appreciate physical expressions of love such as hugs, pats on the back, or holding hands. These gestures show that you care and value their emotions.
- Speak with kindness: When communicating with a feeler, using kind and supportive language is essential. Avoid being overly critical or dismissive of their feelings, even if you don't understand or agree with them.
- Validate their emotions: Feelers may react strongly to situations that thinkers might not fully understand. Validate their feelings and let them know you appreciate their feelings.
- Create a supportive environment: Feelers thrive in supportive and caring environments. Create a safe space where they can express their emotions without fear of judgment or criticism.

Empathy, kindness, and understanding are essential to show care for a feeler. Show that you value their emotions and create a supportive environment in which they can express themselves freely.

Caring is a skill that can be developed. The better you are at it, the more influence you have.

In the next chapter, we will share with you the superpower of learning to clarify. This concept could change your relationships forever.

Note

1. Erik Erikson's Psychosocial Theory was first introduced in his book *Childhood and Society*, published in 1950. The theory has been expanded and revised in subsequent books and articles written by Erikson throughout his career. Some of his other notable works on the subject include *Identity: Youth and Crisis* (1968), *The Life Cycle Completed* (1982), and *Vital Involvement in Old Age* (1986).

6

The Superpower of Clarity

"The clearer you are, the easier it is for people to follow you."
—Minda Zetlin

Communication is a two-way street, and there is a responsibility for both parties to invest in each other to develop a relationship. Clarity is a significant skill set to learn to build relationships that last.

The superpower of clarifying refers to the ability to ask questions or provide information in a way that leads to a greater understanding of a situation. It involves asking the right questions, rephrasing statements, or querying to elicit more accurate responses, and helping others communicate what they are trying to say.

Most people don't do either—asking for clarity or helping people by clarifying, which can cause emotional friction—well.

Clarifying is valuable because it enables individuals to communicate more effectively with others, resolve misunderstandings, and prevent confusion. It is beneficial when there is a need to convey critical information, make decisions, or solve problems.

Because it unlocks people's Communication Code, it has the power to build stronger relationships, as it shows that one is actively listening and interested in understanding the other person's perspective. It can also create a culture of open communication and collaboration. People feel more comfortable expressing their ideas and opinions when they know they will be understood and heard.

In this chapter, you will learn how to clarify well and why it is important to unlocking others' Communication Code.

What Clarity Actually Is

As stated in the Communication Code, clarifying means making a statement or situation less confusing and more clearly understandable. When you share the code word, you ask: "I know I have something important to share; would you take the time to ask great questions so I can get it out? Please know that what I say first won't be where we end up, so be patient with me."

When you clarify, you make something more straightforward, easy to understand, or free of confusion. The clarification process can involve providing additional information, examples, or explanations as well as asking questions or seeking feedback to ensure that the message or data being conveyed is understood correctly.

Most people don't listen to the complete transmission of information before assuming they know what the other person is trying to say and start to either prepare their response, or in the case of extroverts, even complete the sentence for the other person so they can start talking again.

Clarification ensures that everyone is on the same page and that there is no confusion or misunderstanding about a particular subject or issue.

But what if there isn't clarity?

Clarity Matters

Asking for clarity is crucial. One historical blunder is the Treaty of Waitangi, signed in New Zealand in 1840. The treaty was meant to establish a relationship between the British Crown and the indigenous Māori people and to provide a legal framework for the British settlement of New Zealand.

However, the treaty became a source of ongoing conflict and grievance due to several factors, including cultural differences and misunderstandings.

One of the critical issues was the translation of the treaty into Māori. The British officials who drafted the treaty wrote it in English and then had it translated into Māori by a missionary named Henry Williams and his son Edward. However, the Williams's translation was flawed in several ways. For example, the Māori word *kawanatanga* was used to translate the English word *governorship*, but *kawanatanga* did not have the same connotations of sovereignty and authority as "governorship" did in English. Similarly, the Māori word *rangatiratanga* was used to translate the English word *sovereignty*, but *rangatiratanga* referred more to chieftainship and leadership than to the kind of supreme authority that the British Crown was claiming.

As a result of these translation errors, the Māori chiefs who signed the treaty believed they were granting the British Crown limited governorship over the settlers, while retaining their sovereignty and authority over their people and lands. However, the British officials who had drafted the treaty believed they were gaining full sovereignty over New Zealand, and that the Māori chiefs were ceding all their authority to the British Crown.

This miscommunication led to conflicts and wars between the British and the Māori over the following decades, as the Māori sought to protect their rights and lands, and the British sought to impose their authority. The treaty remains a source of controversy and debate in New Zealand today, as Māori continue to seek recognition of their rights and grievances under the treaty and as the country struggles to reconcile its colonial past with its multicultural present.

Communicating with clarity is something both parties are responsible for. If both had asked clarifying questions with humility, genuinely trying to understand the perspective of the other, a lot of pain and hurt would have been avoided.

Clarifying Benefits Everyone

Clarifying ensures that both parties have a shared understanding of a topic or message, and helps to prevent misunderstandings, confusion, and errors. Clarifying is crucial because it helps to avoid miscommunication, build trust, improve accuracy, enhance problem solving, and increase productivity.

Drama occurs daily in most businesses because there is little attempt to understand what the other person is saying. Clarifying what a co-worker wants can help improve communication, job satisfaction, performance, expectations, and engagement, which benefits both the employee and the organization.

Rhett and Mary were working on a project together for their company. Rhett was the project lead, and Mary was a team member. They had a meeting to discuss the project's progress and next steps. During the session, Rhett worked hard to understand what Mary was trying to say. He began to move on until he remembered the Communication Code.

Rhett used the Communication Code to ask Mary to clarify what she shared. He repeated her ideas back to her in his own words and asked if he had understood her correctly.

By the end of the meeting, Rhett and Mary better understood each other's perspectives. They were able to come up with a more comprehensive plan for the project. Rhett thanked Mary for sharing her ideas and encouraged her to continue doing so in the future.

Over the next few weeks, Rhett noticed that Mary's confidence and engagement had increased. She was more willing to share her ideas and suggestions, which led to a more collaborative and innovative work environment. The project was completed successfully, and the entire organization benefited from the team's improved communication and collaboration.

Taking the time to understand it usually leads to better outcomes for the project and the entire organization.

Whom Are You Talking To

As John Dryden says, "Words are but pictures of our thoughts." Knowing the other person well can make those pictures clearer, positively alter the relational dynamics, and lead the other person to levels of peace with you that you may not have thought possible.

Everyone is different. Some people are wired to get to the point and solve problems. They love to collaborate and critique, and believe that is where they add the most value.

What happens when that person wants to know you care or desires to celebrate before getting to collaboration? When people don't communicate effectively, it adds to past frustrations and it adds complexity to the relationship.

Remember to think about whom you are talking to before transmitting your information. What are the relational dynamics already in play? What are their default Communication Codes, and what cipher must you send beforehand?

As mentioned in Chapter 3, our work on the 5 Voices provides a powerful lens to help you understand the personality wiring and default tendencies of the person you seek to communicate with. You have to be intentional, particularly if they are wired very differently to you.

Steve and I are both future-oriented voices, meaning we love to dream about what could be. The only difference is that

I am a feeler and he is a thinker, which means that I am more focused on the relational feelings of others. At the same time, Steve is more focused on logic and reason.

As shared, this difference has led to some epic brother-like battles that eventually led to the creation of this very tool so that you don't have to suffer the same frustrations we have.

How to Clarify Well

There are several strategies to use clarification in communication with other humans effectively.

- Ask questions: Peter Drucker once quipped: "A great question is better than the right answer to the wrong question." One of the simplest ways to clarify a message is to ask questions. This shows that you are actively listening and interested in understanding the other person's perspective. Open-ended questions, such as "What do you mean?" are more beneficial than close-ended questions such as "Did you mean...?" because they encourage the other person to provide more detailed responses.
- Paraphrase: Paraphrasing involves restating the other person's message in your own words. This can confirm that you have understood the message correctly and shows the other person that you are actively listening and engaging in the conversation.
- Use examples: Using examples can help to clarify a message by providing concrete illustrations of abstract concepts or ideas. This can help to make the message more relatable and easier to understand.
- Check for understanding: After a message has been communicated, it's essential to check for understanding by

asking the other person to repeat or summarize the message in their own words. This helps ensure that both parties have a shared experience of the news.

- Be patient: Clarifying can take time, and it's essential to be patient and give the other person enough time to fully express their message. Interrupting or rushing the conversation can prevent effective clarification from occurring.

Active Listening Audit

All of the preceding information is built on solid listening skills. Let's see how good you are at actively listening to others. That is *active*, not *passive*. It means intentionally listening to understand others so that you can clarify what they are saying.

Here is an Active Listening Assessment to help you evaluate your communication skills:

1. How often do you interrupt others when they are speaking?
   a) Never b) Rarely c) Sometimes d) Frequently
2. How often do you ask follow-up questions to clarify someone's point?
   a) Always b) Often c) Sometimes d) Rarely
3. How often do you paraphrase what someone has said to ensure you understand them correctly?
   a) Always b) Often c) Sometimes d) Rarely
4. How often do you avoid multitasking while someone is speaking to you?
   a) Always b) Often c) Sometimes d) Rarely
5. How often do you provide verbal or nonverbal feedback to show you are listening?
   a) Always b) Often c) Sometimes d) Rarely

6. How often do you show empathy and acknowledge the other person's feelings?
   a) Always b) Often c) Sometimes d) Rarely
7. How often do you seek to understand the other person's perspective before expressing your own?
   a) Always b) Often c) Sometimes d) Rarely
8. How often do you avoid jumping to conclusions or making assumptions about what the other person is saying?
   a) Always b) Often c) Sometimes d) Rarely
9. How often do you actively listen to feedback from others without becoming defensive?
   a) Always b) Often c) Sometimes d) Rarely
10. How often do you follow up on conversations with action items or further discussions?
    a) Always b) Often c) Sometimes d) Rarely

Which of the preceding areas need the most work?

Show your results to one person in your life whom you trust will be honest with you. Where do they think you can improve?

Why You Want Others to Clarify

Jake was an employee at an insurance company working on an important project for his boss, Sarah. Jake had been working hard on the project for weeks and was eager to present his ideas to Sarah, but he worried she might not understand his proposal.

So, Jake scheduled a meeting with Sarah to present his ideas and to ask for clarification on a few points. He thought that by clearly understanding what Sarah wanted, he could ensure that his proposal met her expectations.

As Jake began to speak, Sarah interrupted him with critiques and suggestions on improving his proposal. Jake was taken aback. He had expected Sarah to take the time to truly understand what he was saying; instead, she launched immediately into a critique of what she thought he was saying in his proposal.

Feeling discouraged, Jake left the meeting frustrated. He thought Sarah didn't understand his proposal and that his hard work had gone to waste.

On the other hand, Sarah didn't realize that her behavior was causing Jake to feel this way. She thought she was being helpful by offering suggestions and collaborating on the proposal. Still, she didn't understand that Jake needed her to listen and allow Jake to ask his clarifying questions.

Jake talked to Sarah about how her behavior made him feel, and how he needed her to listen and clarify before moving forward. He reminded her that he was "creative," and his ideas were complex but helpful. He just needed the patience to help get them out of his head.

Sarah apologized and promised to change her approach. From that day on, Sarah made a conscious effort to listen and clarify before giving feedback. Jake felt more confident and motivated in his work.

Clarifying Is Your Responsibility

George Bernard Shaw says it best: "The single biggest problem in communication is the illusion that it has taken place."

Clarification is the responsibility of both the sender and the receiver. The sender must provide a cipher, so the receiver understands their intent and desired response. The receiver needs to ask clarifying questions, both to help the sender bring clarity to their ideas, and also to ensure they've genuinely heard what the sender is trying to communicate.

Many people set others up for failure by not sharing the code word they need for clarity. The other side then feels like they let the other person down and begin this awkward stage of not knowing how to ask for clarity.

Therefore, if you are the sender, ask for it. And, if you are the receiver, ask if you can clarify. This is the best way to ensure you are on the same page.

Nancy Duarte says, "Clarity is not just a matter of intelligence or insight; it's a skill, discipline, and commitment. You have to work at it every day, and it's everybody's responsibility to communicate clearly."

Clarification is your responsibility.

In the next chapter, we will dive into the secrets to collaboration and how to do it well. Communication is a lost art, and each of these chapters might help you become stronger in what is difficult to learn.

7 Collaborating to Win

"Collaboration is the fuel that allows common people to attain uncommon results."
—Andrew Carnegie

Collaboration is a competitive advantage.

In the mid-1970s, Steve Jobs and Steve Wozniak worked together to develop and market the first Apple computer, which as we know, revolutionized the personal computer industry. Jobs was the marketing and business visionary, while Wozniak was the technical genius who designed the computer.

Jobs and Wozniak's collaboration was based on mutual respect and complementary skills. They worked together to turn Wozniak's innovative ideas into a powerful product that could be marketed and sold to the masses. Jobs took care of the business side, such as fundraising and marketing. At the same time, Wozniak focused on designing and building a computer.

Their collaboration resulted in the creation of the Apple II, one of the most successful personal computers ever. The Apple II was a game-changer in the industry, offering a user-friendly interface and color graphics unavailable on other personal computers at the time.

Jobs and Wozniak's collaboration also set the stage for Apple's success in the decades to come. The company continued to innovate and release groundbreaking products, such as the Macintosh, iPod, and iPhone, which changed how people use technology.

The story of Jobs and Wozniak's successful collaboration at that point in time is a testament to the power of teamwork and complementary skills. They combined their different strengths to achieve something neither could have accomplished alone.[1]

Effective collaboration is the ability to align complimentary superpowers to create synergistic outcomes. Jobs and Wozniak certainly did this in the beginning.

In this chapter, we will dive in deep into understanding the art and science of collaborating well.

What Does It Mean to Collaborate?

The preceding example is what collaboration is. It means to work jointly on an activity, mainly to produce or create something. When you share the code word, it sounds like this. "I am inviting you to help shape this with me. I want your wisdom and expertise to help make sure we get the best possible outcome."

Leveraging the Communication Code is vital to improve productivity while building relationships. Collaboration can bring fresh perspectives and new ideas to a project, increase efficiency and productivity, and foster a sense of teamwork and shared ownership.

However, collaboration can also be challenging. It requires a willingness to listen and be open to the ideas of others, to be able to negotiate and compromise, and to be able to work effectively as part of a team. It also requires good communication, clear roles and expectations, and a shared understanding of the goals and objectives of the project.

Overall, collaboration is a powerful tool for achieving common goals, promoting innovation and creativity, and improving the overall effectiveness of a project or organization.

The Making of Great Teams

> *"None of us is as smart as all of us."* —*Ken Blanchard*

If you have never experienced a Formula One (F1) race, you should—if only to observe the levels of teamwork.

F1 race teams require high levels of collaboration and coordination to succeed. There are so many variables tied to becoming a dynasty. Here are some of the key ways in which F1 race teams collaborate:

1. Team structure: F1 race teams are divided into various departments: aerodynamics, chassis, power unit, and race operations. Each department has a specific role in developing the car and ensuring it performs well on the track. Each department must collaborate with the other departments to share information and ensure that everyone is working toward the same goal.
2. Data analysis: F1 teams collect vast data during testing and race weekends. The teams' engineers analyze the data to gain insights into the car's performance and make decisions on how to improve it. Effective collaboration is crucial in this process as the data from each department needs to be integrated and analyzed to develop a comprehensive understanding of the car's performance.
3. Pit stops: During races, F1 teams must perform pit stops quickly and efficiently to change tires, refuel, and make necessary repairs. This requires a high level of coordination among the pit crew, mechanics, and the driver to ensure that the pit stop is completed as quickly as possible without making any mistakes.
4. Communication: Effective communication is critical in F1, both during races and outside of them. F1 teams use various communication tools, such as radios, data links, and telemetry, to keep everyone informed and working together toward a common goal.
5. Testing: F1 teams conduct extensive testing to develop and refine their cars. Testing involves the drivers, engineers, and mechanics collaborating to collect data and evaluate the car's performance. The feedback the drivers

provide is critical in this process, as it helps the team identify areas for improvement and develop new strategies for success.

The more complex a process, the healthier collaboration is needed. Collaboration requires a high level of humility. Each team member starts with the assumption that they need the wisdom and expertise of others to win the race.

Blitz

In 2020, we made Bronson Taylor CEO of GiANT. One of his strengths is his style of collaboration—the system of getting things done.

Bronson began to implement his system for getting things done. He began to merge GiANT's flywheel of Communication, Relational Trust, Alignment, Execution, and Capacity with his team system called Blitz.

Blitz is an acronym for Brave Goals, Laser Meetings, Important Projects, Task Lists, and Zero Excuses. It is a weekly system that makes Sprints/Agile look tame.

We have never experienced the amount of productivity with the depths of relationships inside this collaboration process. This codified collaborative process led to healthier relational dynamics inside our team and a dramatic increase in productivity levels. It is phenomenal.

Collaboration is directly tied to communication and relationships, baked in celebration and care. Without these areas, gaining alignment and executing initiatives is much more challenging. Why? Because people like to work with people they want. And if people like other people, they will become more engaged. If people don't like other people, they will become compliant and get very little done.

Collaborative Strength

The Wright brothers, Orville and Wilbur, were not only brothers, but also close collaborators and friends. They had a strong bond and worked together for years to achieve their dream of creating the first powered flight.

Orville and Wilbur were born four years apart and grew up in a close-knit family. They shared a passion for flying and worked tirelessly to achieve their goals. They built their first glider together in 1899. They collaborated on increasingly sophisticated gliders until they reached the first successful powered flight in 1903.

Throughout their partnership, the Wright brothers had a great deal of respect and affection for each other. They complemented each other's skills and were able to work through disagreements and setbacks to achieve their goals. They also had a strong sense of humor and often teased each other as well.

Collaboration happens most effectively when people really like each other. When the relational dynamics are healthy, and each respects the superpowers of the other, something special can happen. That's the GiANT story.

As of this book launch, Steve and I have worked together for a decade. We shared with you our hardships around communication. It is not the easiest when we live across the pond from one another (United Kingdom and United States). Still, it has worked—for 10 years, we have focused on raising liberating leaders in every city and sector, and it has worked. We have collaborated on content, structure, programs, and technology plans.

One of the reasons it has worked is that we have had a vision for something higher than both of us. Our vision, mission, and values have helped keep us together and propel us to higher levels of thinking and work.

Because we have complementary superpowers, collaboration has taken intentionality and time. If we were wired the same way, the relational dynamics would have been less complicated, but the outcome would not have been the same. Our marriages have also been the context for content/tool creation because we are both married to our opposites in terms of personality.

If you hire people like you, then relational dynamics are simple, but the collaborative output of the team will be less than it could be. We need different characters, personalities, and life experiences to build outlier teams.

The opposite is also true.

Examples of Poor Collaboration

When you don't collaborate well with someone, it can harm you and the other person. Here are a few situations that we have seen occur when there is poor collaboration:

- Decreased productivity: When you don't collaborate well with someone, it can lead to inefficiencies and delays in completing tasks. This can decrease productivity for you and the other person and affect the team. It happens all the time.
- Increased stress: Poor collaboration can also lead to increased pressure for both parties. When there is a lack of communication or teamwork, it can create tension and conflict that can be emotionally draining.
- Damaged relationships: When you don't collaborate well with someone, it can damage your relationship. This can lead to resentment, mistrust, and a communication breakdown, making it even harder to work together in the future.

- Negative impact on outcomes: Poor collaboration can ultimately hurt outcomes. When team members don't work together effectively, it can lead to missed deadlines, subpar work, and unsatisfactory results.

These are just a few examples of the ramifications of people not collaborating well.

Collaboration Assessment

This collaboration assessment can be used to evaluate how well two co-workers collaborate:

1. Communication:
   - Does the co-worker communicate clearly and effectively?
   - Does the co-worker listen actively and ask questions to clarify information?
   - Does the co-worker share information on time?
2. Trust:
   - Does the co-worker trust their colleague to complete tasks and projects?
   - Does the co-worker respect their colleague's opinions and ideas?
   - Does the co-worker give credit to their colleague when due?
3. Conflict Resolution:
   - Does the co-worker address conflict professionally and constructively?
   - Does the co-worker actively seek to resolve conflicts rather than avoid them?
   - Does the co-worker compromise and find solutions that benefit both parties?

4. Accountability:
   - Does the co-worker take responsibility for their actions and mistakes?
   - Does the co-worker follow through on commitments and promises?
   - Does the co-worker hold their colleague accountable for their actions?
5. Teamwork:
   - Does the co-worker actively contribute to the team's goals and objectives?
   - Does the co-worker offer support and assistance to their colleague?
   - Does the co-worker promote a positive and collaborative team environment?

Each question can be rated on a scale of 1 to 5, with 1 being poor and 5 being excellent. The scores can then be totaled and compared to an ideal score to assess the level of collaboration between the co-workers. This assessment can be used periodically to track progress and identify areas for improvement in cooperation.

During a business partner intensive, Todd and Brian decided they needed to address some issues. Todd noticed that their collaboration wasn't as effective as possible, and he wasn't sure how to improve it. He agreed to take the Collaboration Assessment with Brian to identify areas of improvement.

Todd and Brian answered each question honestly and discussed their answers in detail. They discovered that communication was vital as both tended to make assumptions and not clarify information. They also found that they had different expectations around accountability, leading to confusion and frustration.

After the assessment, Todd and Brian were able to identify specific actions to improve their collaboration. They agreed to set up regular communication check-ins to ensure they were on the same page and clarify any assumptions. They also created a shared document to track accountability and ensure that tasks were completed on time.

As a result of taking the Collaboration Assessment and implementing changes to their collaborative approach, Todd and Brian could work more effectively together and meet their project deadline. They became adept at using the Communication Code to ensure the right timing to collaborate and critique.

They felt more confident in their ability to collaborate on future projects, and they continued using the assessment to track their progress and make improvements.

Collaboration is the fruit of healthy relational dynamics and effective communication. If collaboration is going well, then your team and/or family is probably winning.

In the next chapter, we will discuss the delicate and important topic of critique. Critiquing can result in so much damage if done poorly. Let's work on getting good at it together.

Note

1. The book *Steve Jobs* was written by Walter Isaacson and published by Simon & Schuster in 2011.

8 How to Critique Without Being Critical

"A well-placed critique can be a catalyst for growth and improvement."
—Albert Einstein

Critique is a formal word that typically refers to a careful judgment in which someone gives an opinion. It means to review or examine something critically. It should not be about finding fault, but rather a process of providing helpful feedback to improve someone's work.

When you share this code word, you say, "I'm inviting you to critique my work; I want you to ask the difficult questions! Do your due diligence—I need to know: why isn't this going to work?"

If you ask to critique something, it might sound like: "Are you okay if I offer some critique? I would love to help you make this better."

A critique can take many forms, but generally it involves identifying the strengths and weaknesses of a work and providing constructive feedback on how it can be improved or why something won't work.

Critiquing can be a valuable tool for helping individuals or groups improve their skills and abilities, and fostering creative and intellectual growth. However, it is crucial that critiques are done constructively and respectfully, and that the person receiving the critique is open to feedback and willing to learn from it.

In this chapter, we will solve a lot of pain by giving you tools on how to critique without being negative—to truly help people by giving it or help you by learning how to receive the critique of others.

The Difference between Critique versus Criticism

A critique is not the same as a criticism, often pointing out flaws and shortcomings. A critique is more of an analysis and evaluation of the work, where the focus is not only on what is wrong, but also on what is right and how it can be improved.

Critique and criticism are similar in that they both involve evaluating and providing feedback on someone's work or actions. However, there are some critical differences between the two:

- Tone and intent: Critique is typically seen as more constructive and helpful, while criticism is often viewed as negative and judgmental. Critique is intended to help the person improve and grow, while criticism can be seen as an attack.
- Focus on the work versus the person: Critique is focused on the work itself, while criticism often becomes personal and attacks the individual. Critique focuses on the areas where improvement can be made, while criticism can be general and vague.
- Level of detail: Critique often involves providing detailed feedback on the work. At the same time, criticism may be more general and less clear.
- Delivery: Critique is often delivered respectfully and empathetically, while criticism can be shown in a harsh or insensitive manner.

Here is a simple summary: Critique is focused on being for someone and helping the person improve their work or specific skill sets. An honest critique of performance helps develop leadership capability.

At the same time, criticism is often negative, and it feels like someone is against you. By providing a constructive critique, you can help the person grow and improve while avoiding the negative connotations that come with criticism.

This chapter will focus on two aspects of critique: How to deliver critique well, and how to receive critique well.

How to Deliver Critique Well

Critiquing is a skill that, with more practice, will improve your relational dynamics. We want to give you some practical ways to see improvement through the following concepts.

> *"The art of critique lies in offering guidance, not delivering judgment."*
> *—Vincent van Gogh*

The Constructive Method

The best method to critique without being critical is to approach the critique constructively and supportively. Here are some tips on how to do that:

1. Start with positive feedback: Begin by highlighting what the person did well or what you appreciated about their work. This sets a positive tone for the conversation and makes it easier for the person to receive feedback.
2. Be specific: When giving feedback, be clear about what you liked and what could be improved. Avoid general statements like "This is terrible" or "You're doing it wrong." Instead, point out specific examples of what can be improved and offer suggestions for how to do so.
3. Use "I" statements: Use "I" statements when providing feedback, such as, "I think it would be helpful if...." or,

"I noticed that...." This takes the focus off the person and puts it on the specific behavior or issue that needs improvement.

4. Ask for their perspective: Ask the person for their thoughts on the feedback you've given. This can help create a dialogue and allow them to respond and share their ideas.
5. Follow up: Check in with the person to see how they're doing and whether they've made progress on improving the issue. This shows you care about their growth and development and are invested in their success.
6. Offer suggestions: When providing feedback, offer suggestions for improvement. Don't just point out problems without providing potential solutions. This can help people feel empowered to make changes and improve their work.
7. End with encouragement: End your critique positively by expressing confidence in the person's ability to improve and offering encouragement for future efforts.

Elizabeth and Shawna worked at a marketing agency and often collaborated on projects. Shawna approached Elizabeth for help on a project she was working on. Elizabeth agreed to review Shawna's work and provide feedback.

After reviewing Shawna's work, Elizabeth identified a few areas where Shawna could improve. Instead of telling her what was wrong, Elizabeth asked Shawna if she was open to collaboration and critique. She started by acknowledging Shawna's strengths and positive contributions to the project. Then, she provided specific feedback on areas where Shawna could improve. Finally, Elizabeth ended the critique by reaffirming Shawna's potential and the value of her work.

At first, Shawna was a bit defensive and felt discouraged by the feedback. However, Elizabeth listened actively and responded empathetically, acknowledging Shawna's hard work on the project. Elizabeth reminded her of the Communication Code and her intent for the critique.

Over time, Shawna began to incorporate Elizabeth's feedback and saw improvements in her work. She also appreciated Elizabeth's approach to critique, which was always respectful and constructive. This experience helped strengthen their working relationship and build mutual respect and trust.

By providing specific feedback and ending on a positive note, Elizabeth delivered her critique in a supportive and helpful way.

Very few people love having their work critiqued. However, when critique is delivered constructively and sensitively, it creates the context for powerful collaboration.

Tone and Tact

Tone is how you say things, like the attitude or feeling you convey when you speak or write. It's like the "vibe" you give off with your words, whether you sound happy, sad, angry, or sarcastic. Your tone can affect how people understand what you're saying, and it's essential to be aware of it to communicate effectively.

Tact is the ability to say or do something that doesn't offend or upset people. It's about communicating or handling a situation without being too harsh or insensitive. Tactful people have a knack for navigating tricky or sensitive situations without causing unnecessary drama or hurt feelings. Think of it as telling someone the truth without being rude or hurting their feelings.

It is said that tone makes up 35% of how people experience our communication, while the rest is 10% words and

55% body language. The words can be spot on, but they won't hear what we are trying to say if the tone is wrong.

A person who understands their tone and tact and uses it well will have a better chance to crack through the relational code of another person and provide a critique that helps. Conversely, if people don't understand how they sound or look, they are most likely unaware of why effective communication remains elusive.

Allison had always been a caring and nurturing wife, doing everything she could to ensure her husband, Stephan, was happy and content. But lately, Stephan seemed to have taken her for granted, ignoring her needs and desires and only focusing on her shortcomings.

One evening, as Allison was preparing dinner, Stephan walked into the kitchen and began to critique her cooking, thinking he was collaborating. He commented on the seasoning, temperature, and presentation using a sharp and critical tone to address her. Allison felt a pang of hurt and disappointment, but she tried to remain composed.

However, Stephan's criticisms continued throughout the meal, from how Allison had set the table to the color of the tablecloth. He seemed oblivious to her feelings, and did not consider the effort and care she had put into the evening.

Allison tried to communicate her hurt to Stephan. Still, he dismissed her feelings, telling her she was being "way too sensitive" and that he was only trying to help her improve. But his words only made things worse, and Allison felt more and more unappreciated.

As the weeks passed, Stephan's criticisms grew more frequent, and his tone became increasingly harsh. Allison began to dread spending time with him, and the once-loving couple began to drift apart. Eventually, Allison realized she could no longer tolerate the constant criticism and confronted Stephan about his behavior.

In their heart-to-heart conversation, Allison explained how Stephan's words had made her feel, eroded her self-confidence, and left her feeling unloved and unsupported. Stephan was taken aback by her words, realizing for the first time how his actions had hurt his wife.

The Other Side of You

This story brings up a challenging question: do you know what it is like to be on the other side of you?

Do you know what you look like when you critique someone else? Body language is crucial in how the other person receives your critique.

Even if the words are constructive, if the body language is hostile or aggressive, it can make the other person feel attacked or defensive. For example, crossing arms, leaning forward aggressively, or rolling eyes while giving feedback can make the other person feel like they're being judged or rebuked. Eye rolling should be banned, by the way.

On the other hand, maintaining open body language, such as facing the person directly, maintaining eye contact, and using a calm tone of voice, can help the other person feel like they're being listened to and respected, even if the feedback is not entirely positive. Therefore, being mindful of body language is crucial when giving critique to someone else.

This leads us to share some important lessons:

1. Critique without invitation will likely be experienced as criticism.
2. When a thinker tries to collaborate without the clear use of the Communication Code, the message will often be experienced as criticism.
3. Offering critique when relational dynamics are off will invariably be experienced as criticism.

Critique with Liberation in Mind

When you provide High support and challenge to another person, you can expect positive and productive results. High support means showing the other person that you believe in them and are there to help them succeed. This can increase confidence, motivation, and a sense of belonging, making the person more receptive to new challenges.

> *"Criticism, like rain, should be gentle enough to nourish a man's growth without destroying his roots."* —*Frank A. Clark*

High challenge means that you are pushing the other person to step outside of their comfort zone and take on new opportunities. This can help them develop new skills, learn new things, and achieve their full potential. When you combine High support and High challenge, the person feels supported and challenged, which can increase engagement, motivation, and productivity.

The combination of High support and High challenge can lead to a positive working relationship based on mutual respect, trust, and a shared commitment to success. This can lead to improved performance, growth, and achieving excellent results together.

The truth is that people need to know that you are for them, and they must have experienced it in the past to receive your critique well.

How to Receive Critique Well

Tracy was the CEO of a rapidly growing startup. She always welcomed feedback from her team, including her chairman, Robert. Tracy genuinely appreciated Robert's insight and guidance, unlike some CEOs who might get defensive or angry when receiving feedback.

One day, Robert pulled Tracy aside after a meeting to give her some constructive criticism about her leadership style. He noted that while she was doing a great job overall, she could benefit from being more decisive and taking more risks. Tracy listened attentively to his feedback, nodding her head and taking notes.

Instead of feeling attacked or criticized, Tracy felt grateful for Robert's input. She knew that he had a wealth of experience in the business world, and even though he didn't use the Communication Code, she was well aware of it and had learned how to receive the critique. She knew the feedback came from a place of care and concern for the company's success because Robert had always shown that he was fighting for her highest possible good.

Tracy took Robert's feedback to heart and made a conscious effort to be more decisive in her decision-making and to take calculated risks when appropriate. Over time, she saw the benefits of this approach as the company continued to grow and thrive under her leadership.

Tracy's willingness to receive critique from Robert, and her openness to learning and growing as a leader, helped her become a more effective CEO and led to her company's success. She continually shows a positive attitude toward feedback, and her willingness to act based on it sets an excellent example for the rest of her team.

How Thinkers Receive Critique

Thinkers open to receiving critique typically approach it with a positive and growth-oriented mindset. They recognize that feedback, even if it's negative, can help them improve and reach their full potential.

It is almost like they hold their ideas away from their heart and allow others to shoot holes in their idea, knowing that others are trying to improve them. In essence, they don't take the feedback as personally as feelers.

When receiving critique, thinkers listen attentively, ask clarifying questions, and take notes. They don't get defensive or dismissive, even if the feedback is hard to hear. Instead, they try to understand the other person's perspective and see it as an opportunity to learn and grow.

Thinkers need to be able to critique the critique to both fully understand the challenge and push back if they disagree with it. They must also respect the competence and expertise of those who critique their work.

After receiving critique, thinkers reflect on what they've heard. They might seek additional feedback or research to gain more insight. They use the feedback as a starting point for making changes or improvements and track their progress over time.

How Feelers Receive Critique

For feelers, receiving critique can be especially difficult. It's easy for them to take things personally and let them affect their self-worth. They are different than thinkers. Feelers take their ideas and put them over their heart—they make them personal. Therefore, when people shoot holes in their ideas, they see blood because they truly feel wounded.

There are ways, however, that feelers can protect themselves while still being open to constructive criticism. We call these methods "putting on your Kevlar."

First, feelers need to take care of themselves emotionally. People must learn to manage their emotions, so others don't have to work them for them. This will help them to approach the critique from a more centered and grounded place.

Second, feelers should try to separate their work from their sense of self-worth. They should remind themselves that critique is about their work, not about them as a person. This cannot be easy, but they need to recognize that their work doesn't define their worth as human beings.

Third, feelers should seek to understand the other person's perspective by asking questions and seeking clarification. This will help them to see things from a different angle and to know where the feedback is coming from. They should take notes and reflect on the feedback later, looking for ways to incorporate it into their work.

Finally, feelers should seek support from trusted friends or colleagues when needed. Talking through their feelings and concerns with others can help them to see things more objectively and to process the feedback more effectively.

Feelers must ask themselves if they believe the person offering the critique is truly for them and want to fight for their highest possible good. Assuming the answer is yes, this is another positive lens that helps them engage with the critique.

By taking these steps, feelers can protect themselves emotionally while being open to constructive criticism. They can use the feedback to learn and grow without letting it affect their sense of self-worth.

Making Critique Work for You, Not against You

Another story from Apple occurred in the late 1990s. Apple was struggling, and Steve Jobs had just returned to the company as CEO. Jobs was known for his exacting standards and was unafraid to critique his employees' work. One of those employees was Jony Ive, who had just joined Apple as a senior designer.

Ive had designed a new product, the iMac G3, which he was very proud of. However, when he showed it to Jobs, Jobs was not impressed. He criticized the design, saying it was too bulky and lacked the elegance Apple was known for.

Ive was devastated by the critique, but he took Jobs's feedback to heart. He returned to the drawing board and came up with a new design that was sleeker, more elegant, and more in line with Apple's design philosophy. The new design was a hit, and the iMac G3 became one of Apple's most successful products.

Jobs continued to critique Ive's work over the years. Still, he also recognized Ive's talent and allowed him to design products that were true to his vision. Ive went on to create many of Apple's most iconic products, including the iPod, iPhone, and iPad.

While receiving feedback on our work can be difficult, it can also help us grow and improve. Jobs was not consistent with High support and High challenge, according to Walter Isaacson's book *Steve Jobs*. However, his critique of Ive's work helped him to develop a better design and, ultimately, contributed to Apple's success.

Learning to Love Critique

The best way to take critique is not to take the feedback personally. Critique is simply someone else's opinion on improving something.

Learning to love critique can be a challenging process, but here are some tips that may help:

- Embrace a growth mindset: Start by reframing how you view critique. Instead of seeing it as an attack on your abilities, view it as an opportunity to learn and grow. Adopting a growth mindset can help you to see critique as a valuable tool for self-improvement.

- Separate critique from criticism: It's essential to understand that critique is not the same thing as criticism. Critique is the feedback intended to help you improve, whereas criticism is often negative and unconstructive. You can focus on constructive input by learning to distinguish between the two.
- Seek feedback: The more you receive feedback, the easier it can become to learn to love it. Seek feedback from colleagues, mentors, friends, and family members you trust to provide honest feedback. The more you receive feedback, the more comfortable you become with the process.
- Practice active listening: When receiving feedback, it's crucial to actively listen to what the other person is saying. This means fully engaging with the feedback and asking questions for clarification. By actively listening, you can better understand the feedback and its potential to help you improve.
- Focus on the positive: It's essential to focus on the positive aspects of critique. Instead of dwelling on the negative feedback, focus on the areas where you can improve and the growth potential. This can help you to view critique as an opportunity for self-improvement and growth rather than a negative experience.

It is important to listen to the critique and not challenge its accuracy or veracity at that moment. If someone is brave enough to bring challenge and critique, there is truth in what they say, even if it's not 100% accurate. Once you have had the chance to reflect and engage with the critique, you can go back to the person and ask clarifying questions or challenge their critique.

Critique can be unbelievably helpful or extremely damaging based on past relational dynamics, and the tone and tact of delivery. Here are some key chapter points worth remembering as you learn to critique well.

1. "Critique without invitation will likely be experienced as criticism."
2. "When a thinker tries to collaborate without clear use of the Communication Code, the message will often be experienced as criticism."
3. "Offering critique when relational dynamics are off will invariably be experienced as criticism."
4. "When you are secure and confident, you can take critique much easier as you realize you have nothing to prove, lose, or hide."

The goal is to critique with the highest good in your mind for the other person. Ensure they know you are for them, and your critique will improve.

In the next chapter, we will progress into putting all of these concepts together to become a proper people whisperer.

9 People Whispering

At this point in the book, you should be able to:

- Understand the relational dynamics between you and at least one other person.
- Be aware of any historical negativities or power dynamics from you to them.
- Gauge your leadership style of liberating, dominating, protecting, or abdicating.
- Comprehend your communication style of whether you tend to critique, collaborate, clarify, care, or celebrate.

This chapter is designed to put it all together—to fully understand how to unlock the relational dynamics between you and at least one other person. Over time, this should lead you to work on the next relationship and then the next.

We hope you will be a master people whisperer. A people whisperer is self-aware, understands complex relational dynamics, and can consistently choose the correct communication code.

Those who can connect well with others can change almost anything.

Deciding to Change

Ingrid had always prided herself on her honesty and straightforwardness. She was the kind of person who never sugarcoated anything and had no patience for people who did. So, when her friend Maria would come to her with a problem, Ingrid would immediately offer her opinion, even if it was critical.

But over time, Ingrid noticed that Maria was becoming more distant. She seemed to be avoiding Ingrid, and when they did spend time together, the conversations were stilted and awkward.

One day, Ingrid decided to confront Maria about it. "What's going on? Are you mad at me or something?" she asked.

Maria sighed. "It's not that I'm mad at you, Ingrid. It's just that sometimes it feels like you're always criticizing me. I appreciate your honesty, but sometimes I need you to listen and be there for me without judging."

Ingrid was taken aback. She had never realized that her critique was making it difficult for Maria to be friends with her. But as she thought about it more, she began to see how her behavior might come across as harsh and unsympathetic.

Determined to make things right, Ingrid turned to the Communication Code. She realized that Maria needed her to clarify before critiquing. So the next time Maria came to her with a problem, Ingrid asked more open-ended questions to better understand the situation before offering her opinion. She also made a conscious effort to show Maria that she cared about her and valued their friendship.

It was challenging for Ingrid to change her approach. She had to remind herself to clarify before critiquing constantly, and it wasn't easy to hold back her opinions at times. But as she began to see the positive changes in her friendship with Maria, she knew it was worth the effort.

Ingrid's self-awareness process led to a breakthrough in their friendship. Maria began to open up to Ingrid more, and their conversations became more meaningful and enjoyable. Ingrid learned that being honest doesn't always mean being critical and that sometimes the best thing she could do for her friend was to listen and offer support.

Ingrid's newfound respect for Maria's perspective led to a deeper understanding and appreciation of their differences.

They both realized that they could learn from each other and that their friendship was richer and deeper.

Use the Code Word

We have given you clues on how to unlock relationships. The code words—*celebrate*, *care*, *clarify*, *collaborate*, and *critique*—are the needs and desired expectations of the other person.

Asking for the code word is them giving you the clue to unlock the relationship or improve your communication.

Conversely, when you give the other person your code word, you are helping them become more self-aware and giving them skills to communicate well with others in their life.

Honor others by asking what code word they want from you.

Rachel had been working hard on a project but was a bit behind. She shared her worries with her co-worker Chandra. Chandra had become adept at using the Communication Code and asked Rachel, "What do you need from me right now—clarification, care, or collaboration?"

She knew it wasn't a time to celebrate and didn't need her critique. Rachel thought momentarily and replied, "I would appreciate it if you would collaborate with me to help get this project back on track." Chandra replied, "Absolutely, Rachel. I can see how much effort you're putting into this project, and I'm here to support you in any way I can."

Rachel felt relieved and thankful for Chandra's willingness to collaborate with her. She said, "Thank you, Chandra. It's so easy to communicate with you. I can always count on you to understand my needs."

Please help others by telling them what code word you want from them.

Kevin felt proud of himself after closing a big sale for the company. He knew his boss, Javier, would be happy to hear the news, but he wasn't sure how to ask him to celebrate without sounding pushy or demanding.

Using the Communication Code, Kevin started by sharing his expectations and explaining why celebrating his success was essential to him. He said, "Javier, I'm excited about this sale I just closed. It was a big win; I feel I've been progressing lately. Celebrating this success quickly would help me stay motivated for future sales."

Javier listened carefully, appreciating Kevin's honesty and enthusiasm. He replied, "I'm proud of you, Kevin. You've been working hard, and this sale is a great accomplishment. Let's talk about how we can celebrate and recognize your success."

They went to lunch and celebrated it, and that gave Kevin a chance to feel that his boss was for him. Kevin used the time to plan how to keep growing the business strategically. He felt like Javier was not only for him but was an advocate for him.

Using the Communication Code, Kevin could express his expectations clearly and respectfully. This allowed Javier to understand what was important to Kevin and work with him to create a plan for celebrating his success, even though it wasn't the way Javier celebrated personally.

What Do They Want?

The only way to understand what others want is to understand who the other person is. Here are some practical ways to do that:

1. What is their historical pattern?
2. How are they wired?

3. What clues are they giving you?
4. What code word are they giving?

What Do You Want?

Wants are expectations. The Communication Code is a system for sharing expectations. What is it that you want from someone else in a specific situation? Here are practical ways to figure out what you want:

1. Choose three relationships in your life (at work or home).
2. Think of the last significant conversation you had with each.
3. Related to the 5 code words *(celebrate, care, clarify, collaborate,* or *critique)*, what did you desire from them?
4. Did they know that?

Know Your Default Pattern

Which of the code words do you tend to give to others?

- Do you tend to critique first?
- Do you try to collaborate often, even when the other person doesn't want it?
- Do you provide care to everyone as your first default?
- Are you a celebrator of anything, anytime, anywhere?
- Are you good at clarifying before moving on to other code words?

Each of us tends to have two default tendencies that we use in every relationship. Typically, we are unaware of this reality, which means that we could be undermining our influence with others without realizing it—wondering why the relationship isn't very healthy.

Steve has a tendency, historically, to collaborate and then critique. His intent is good; he enjoys helping people solve issues, especially relational dynamics. That allows his skills to be used. Over time, however, Steve has realized that the other person may want to know he cares and to listen appropriately first, or even clarify what they are saying and then ask if it is okay to collaborate or critique.

Jeremie tends to want to celebrate and/or collaborate. While his intent is also good, he can impose his ideas and excitement on the other person without realizing what they may be asking for. He then turns on his firehose of exciting ideas, which can overwhelm the other person, leaving them not knowing what to do with the conversation.

Interestingly, what we give is not the same as what we want. Most people are accidental in their communication; their intent is good and they are trying to help, but often they end up getting it wrong by not using the correct code word. When you stop and think about who you are talking to and what they might want, you are more prone to connect to the other person more appropriately and become more self-aware.

The Communication Code is a cheat sheet for building stronger relationships.

Reading Others Well

To become an expert in relational dynamics, you must learn to read people well. Reading people well means understanding and interpreting their nonverbal cues, such as body language, facial expressions, and tone of voice. It involves observing and analyzing a person's behavior, emotions, and thoughts without relying solely on their words.

People who are good at reading others can pick up on subtle signals and use them to gain insights into their moods, intentions, and personality. For example, they may notice if someone is uncomfortable or nervous based on their body language, eye contact, and speech patterns.

Reading people well can help you connect with others more effectively, build trust, and make better decisions based on a complete understanding of the situation. Here is a practical list that might be helpful for you to consider as you read someone else:

- Observe body language: Pay attention to the nonverbal cues of the people in the room, such as facial expressions, posture, and gestures. These can reveal a lot about their mood and attitude toward the situation.
- Listening ears: Listen to what people are saying and how they are saying it. The tone of voice, speed of speech, and choice of words can indicate emotions and attitudes.
- Be aware of the environment: Take note of the physical setting and the context of the situation, such as the lighting, temperature, and seating arrangements. This can affect people's behavior and mood.
- Look for group dynamics: Observe the interactions between individuals and the group. Who is speaking, who is listening, and who is engaged or disengaged? This can give you an idea of the power dynamics and the level of cohesion in the group.
- Ask questions: When appropriate, ask open-ended questions to gauge people's perspectives and feelings on a particular topic. This can help you better understand them.

Rod was a seasoned executive who had increased his influence over several decades. Throughout his career, he developed a reputation as a skilled communicator adept at reading people well.

One of the critical factors that set Rod apart was his active listening skills. He made a habit of hearing what people were saying and paying close attention to their tone of voice and body language. He would often reflect on what he had heard to ensure he understood it correctly and to show the other person that he was listening.

Over time, he added the Communication Code to his communication tools, making him more effective and quicker. Using this Communication Code, Rod could adapt his communication style to meet others where they were, and build strong relationships based on trust and mutual understanding. He established himself as a respected leader by demonstrating that he understood their needs and concerns.

Another way that Rod was able to read people well was by understanding their personality types. He had studied various personality frameworks, such as Myers-Briggs Type Indicator (MBTI), which helped him recognize different personality traits in others. However, he eventually added the 5 Voices, which made Myers-Briggs even more powerful. This allowed him to anticipate how people might react in certain situations and adjust his approach accordingly.

The next challenge for Rod is learning to apprentice others on his people-whispering skills, which will be the legacy he leaves for many.

Rod can establish a culture of openness and collaboration, in which people feel heard and valued, and everyone works together to achieve common goals. Rod is an excellent example of a people whisperer.

How far away are you?

People Whispering Assessment

Let's see how close you are to becoming a people whisperer. This assessment uses a Likert scale to indicate your level of agreement with each statement on a scale of 1 (strongly disagree) to 5 (strongly agree). Write your answers next to each question.

1. I am a good listener and pay close attention to what others say. ___
2. I can pick up on subtle changes in tone of voice and body language. ___
3. I am skilled at anticipating how others might react in different situations based on their personality. ___
4. I can adjust my communication style to meet the needs of different people. ___
5. I am able to build strong relationships based on trust and mutual understanding. ___
6. I can navigate complex interpersonal dynamics and resolve conflicts effectively. ___
7. I am able to inspire and motivate others to achieve common goals. ___
8. I can provide constructive feedback and coaching that helps people grow and develop. ___
9. I am able to lead by example and set a positive tone for the team or organization. ___
10. I am committed to continuous learning and growth as a leader. ___

Scoring:

- 1–10: You may not possess the skills to be a people whisperer. Consider improving your listening skills and learning more about personality types and communication styles.

- 11–20: You have some of the foundational skills needed to be a people whisperer, but may need to work on building stronger relationships and developing better conflict resolution skills.
- 21–30: You have many critical skills needed to be a people whisperer and likely have some experience building strong relationships and leading others effectively.
- 31–50: You have the skills and experience to be a highly effective people whisperer and likely have a track record of success in building and leading high-performing teams.

Note: This assessment is just a starting point, and should be used for self-reflection and growth. It's essential to continue learning and developing your leadership skills, even if you score highly on this assessment.

Advanced Learning

At the beginning of this book, we discussed communication as being far more than the transmission of information. For effective communication, the sender of the information has to give the receiver clues as to their intent and desired response. Communication is a repeating two-way transmission and receiving process where two people consistently hear each other.

A people whisperer is someone adept at breaking down relational dynamics in an instance.

In the *Sherlock Holmes* movies starring Robert Downey Jr., there are several scenes where he analyzes a situation before it happens. One such scene is in the second movie when Holmes and his partner Dr. Watson are investigating a series of bombings that seem to be connected to their arch-nemesis, Professor Moriarty.

While discussing the case, Holmes begins to analyze their actions' potential outcomes and consequences, considering how Moriarty might react to their investigation. He visualizes different scenarios, explaining the possible results and planning his response accordingly. As he lays them out, they slow down in his mind so he can process them and prepare.

This type of strategic thinking is also vital for people adept at reading others, or people whisperers. By taking the time to understand the other person's personality and communication style, you can anticipate how they might react in a given situation.

For example, suppose a people whisperer knows someone who is particularly sensitive to criticism. In that case, they can adjust their communication style to provide feedback in a constructive, supportive way rather than critical feedback. Or, if they know that someone tends to get defensive in certain situations, they can approach the conversation in a way that is nonconfrontational, and allows the other person to feel heard and valued.

In much the same way that Holmes analyzes the potential outcomes of his actions, People Whisperers can anticipate how their communication and actions might be perceived by others and adjust accordingly. This level of emotional intelligence allows them to easily navigate complex social situations, building solid and positive relationships with those around them.

When you add the Communication Code to this skill set, you can use this same type of thinking to see the relational dynamics of others and adjust their communication style to build stronger, more positive relationships.

Over time, people whisperers become unconsciously competent. In Malcom Gladwell's language, their blink becomes more and more accurate over time.

People whisperers are great at equipping others with the tools they need to address their specific communication challenges.

Team Whispering

For those working inside a team dynamic or even leading a team, you can be as effective with a team as you can be with a person.

Effective communication is essential for any team to work together successfully. Here are some tips for teams to communicate more effectively:

- Set clear expectations: Teams should set clear expectations for communication from the outset, including when and how team members will communicate with each other.
- Choose the proper communication channels: Different communication channels may be appropriate for different situations. For example, email may be best for communicating information or quick celebrations. At the same time, instant messaging or video conferencing may be more suitable for quick questions or brainstorming sessions.
- Be clear and concise: Team members should aim to be clear and concise in their communication, avoiding jargon and unnecessary details.
- Listen actively: Listening is just as essential as speaking. Team members should listen actively to what others are saying, ask questions, and clarify misunderstandings.

- Schedule regular check-ins: Regular check-ins can help teams stay on track and address any issues before they become more significant problems.
- Use visual aids: Visual aids like diagrams, charts, and images can help convey complex information more clearly.
- Provide feedback: Team members should provide feedback to each other to help improve communication and identify areas for improvement.

Effective communication requires a combination of clear expectations, active listening, having a communication toolkit, and providing regular feedback.

Becky was known for her exceptional people skills and communication abilities. She led a team of six members, who were all highly skilled individuals, but often had their priorities and ideas, which made it difficult to align them toward a common goal.

Becky knew that effective communication was critical to her team's success. So she introduced them to the "Communication Code," which became a tool to help her lead them more effectively.

With the Communication Code in place, Becky clarified each team member's expectations and ensured everyone was on the same page. She encouraged her team to use the code words to signify their needs and expectations, which made it easier to understand each other and work together.

For example, when one team member felt overwhelmed or needed help, they would say, "Clarify before collaborating, but I do need help," to let others know how they needed assistance.

Becky also learned to share her expectations for the team's communication, such as telling her team it was okay to critique something she was working on and that they didn't need to worry about retribution. She emphasized the importance of active listening and encouraged team members to ask questions and seek clarification.

Thanks to Becky's leadership and use of the Communication Code, her team became more efficient and productive even though they were sometimes hard to manage.

We have had the privilege of working inside organizations of all shapes and sizes. We also have the chance to partner with coaches and consultants globally, which means we experience or hear hundreds of stories annually around relational dynamics. It is our business.

We hope these stories are helpful. Before we move on to the next chapter of deciding if the relationships are worth it, we want to inspire you on what not to do. Know that we change the names of the participants. Our goal is not to judge, but to use the stories to help you improve.

Don't Be That Person

Oh, Brady. Brady worked at a regional manufacturing company. He had worked there for over 15 years and had loose ties to the family that owned it. That is why he was given a management role.

Brady was tasked with leading a team of talented engineers and project managers on a project. His boss didn't want to put Brady in a leadership role, but had no choice because the family wanted it to happen.

Unfortunately, Brady was utterly clueless regarding communication, understanding personalities, and building trust with his team members. It didn't help that they didn't believe he was competent.

To make matters worse, Brady often critiqued team members without seeking clarification, leaving people frustrated and unsure of how to move forward. People found ways to work around him, and the team struggled to collaborate effectively. Despite feedback from team members and his superiors, Brady failed to see the error of his ways.

As time went on, people grew increasingly unhappy with Brady's leadership. Team members felt undervalued and unappreciated, and morale hit an all-time low. There was talk about bringing in GiANT to help him by going through a leader intensive. However, no one wanted to invest time in him by this point because they didn't think he was responsive enough to change.

Eventually, Brady left the company. It was said that his team threw a celebration lunch after he was gone, which is never good to hear.

Brady was in over his head, and instead of asking for help, he doubled down on his ineffective style. Whatever the opposite of a people whisperer is, Brady represented that. He, unfortunately, was a "people repeller."

Brady's story is a cautionary tale about the importance of effective communication and leadership. It shows that without these skills, a leader can quickly lose the trust and respect of their team, and ultimately fail to achieve their goals.

Now that we have looked at how to be a people whisperer, we'll review in the next chapter whether or not it is worth investing in the people on the other side of you. As we do, let's also think about whether it is worth other people investing in you.

10

Is It Worth It?

"The best investment you can make in life is the investment in relationships."
—Stephen Covey

Building and maintaining a relationship is hard work. Learning to understand relational dynamics and crack communication codes takes time and intentionality. Every relationship is complex and requires a unique code to unlock it fully. If you are not fully committed to making a communication breakthrough in the relationship, it won't happen.

Good intentions are sadly not enough to crack the Communication Code; you need tools, patience, and persistence. Learning to crack communication codes takes time. There are multiple combinations of codes in almost every relationship. It would help if you were committed to breaking the code to experience real breakthroughs with others.

If you are not proficient in cracking codes or don't have the patience to do so, you will tend not to try.

Either way, there is a prize and a price for unlocking the relational communication codes of others. Some relationships are worth fighting for, even if they hurt a bit. Some relationships aren't worth investing in, even if they make you happy. Some relationships are worth the pain because they teach us much about understanding the other person. You must decide how much time, energy, and effort you give to any relationship.

"The price of anything is the amount of life you exchange for it."—Henry David Thoreau

Here are a few relational techniques you can use to evaluate your level of being all in on your relationships.

The Relational Prize Test

Let's unpack our top relationships and run each person through this gauntlet of questions to help us review the strengths of our current relationships and if we should spend more time unlocking them. Choose a number from 1–10 (10 being the highest) based on a relationship's strength. You can take one relationship through each of these and tally your score.

1. Reciprocal relationship: How much is the other person willing to reciprocate and invest in you 1–10_____.

   Advice: Avoid one-sided relationships where you are doing all the work.
2. Compatibility: How similar are the other person's values, goals, and interests to yours 1–10_____.

   Advice: This will create a stronger bond and make it easier to maintain the relationship over time.
3. Communication review: How easy is the communication between you and the other person? 1–10_____.

   Advice: Invest in relationships where healthy communication is present.
4. Positivity percentage: How good do you feel when you have been with this person for any time? 1–10_____.

   Advice: Invest in relationships where the positive interactions outweigh the negative ones.
5. Growth guide: How committed is the other person to their growth and development as well as yours 1–10_____.

   Advice: This will make the relationship more fulfilling.
6. Trust test: How trustworthy is this person 1–10_____.

   Advice: Invest in relationships where trust is present.
7. Happiness factor: How enjoyable is this relationship 1–10_____.

   Advice: Invest in relationships that bring you joy, happiness, and fulfillment.

Add all scores together, divide by 7, and multiply by 10 to get your Relational Prize score. If you score 75–100, then your relationship is solid and reasonable to build upon. If your score is 50–75, then there is a lot of work to be done, and you will need to work with this person to get your scores to higher levels. If your score is 50 or below, you might consider getting professional counseling to help this relationship reach a higher level of relational trust.

The relational prize test can quickly tell you how to invest in the person appropriately.

Evaluating Relationships

Whether or not a relationship is worth it is a subjective question that depends on many different factors around your preferences, goals, and values. Here is a more traditional way to evaluate whether a relationship is worth it or not:

1. Emotional connection: Is the relationship fulfilling? Does it provide emotional support, companionship, and a sense of belonging? If not, you must work to get it to that level.
2. Personal growth: Does this relationship push you to grow mentally, emotionally, or spiritually so that you become the best version of yourself? A great relationship can help you become whom you have always wanted. An excellent evaluation is this—do they make you better?
3. Desire for shared experiences: Relationships are full of shared experiences. One evaluation question to use is: do you want to continue to experience things together? They may be someone you are constantly embarrassed by or frustrated with, which might lead you to decide not to invest more time. The same is valid with those you look forward to sharing experiences with.

4. Willingness to sacrifice: A relationship may require you to make sacrifices, compromise more often than not, and work through challenges. Are you willing to put in the effort that this relationship requires?
5. Compatibility: Compatibility is crucial for a healthy and successful relationship. If you don't click with the other person, it may lead to conflicts and dissatisfaction.

Kate had been friends with Amelia since they were kids. They went to the same school, participated in extracurricular activities, and attended the same university.

However, as they grew older, Kate began to notice that Amelia had become increasingly hostile and critical. She always complained about something, whether it was the weather, her job, or her relationships.

Kate had always been optimistic and found it exhausting to be around Amelia's constant negativity. She had tried to talk to Amelia about it before. Still, whenever she brought up the subject, Amelia would get defensive and shut down the conversation.

One day, Kate decided to evaluate whether it was worth investing more in her friendship with Amelia. She sat down and listed the pros and cons of their friendship.

On the one hand, they had been friends for years, and Amelia had been there for Kate during some tough times. On the other hand, Amelia's negativity brought her down and made her feel drained.

As Kate looked at her list, she realized that the cons outweighed the pros. She couldn't continue to invest in a friendship draining her energy and bringing her down. She knew it wouldn't be easy to distance herself from Amelia, but she also knew it was the right thing to do for her well-being.

Kate decided to talk to Amelia again and explain how she was feeling. She was nervous, but knew being honest with her friend was important. To her surprise, Amelia listened and apologized for her behavior. She admitted that she had been through a tough time and promised to be more positive and supportive.

Kate was relieved and grateful that Amelia had listened to her. She realized that investing in their friendship was worth it, but only if they could be honest and supportive. From that day on, their friendship improved, and Kate felt happier and more energized than ever.

Whether a relationship is worthwhile depends on your priorities, desires, and compatibility with the other person. A relationship can be fulfilling and rewarding if it provides emotional connection, personal growth, and shared experiences. You are willing to make sacrifices and work through challenges with them.

Consider how they respond to you to determine if a relationship is worth it.

Resistant or Responsive

A resistant person is someone who, out of pride or insecurity, is opposed to you or prevents the resolution of any issue out of their immaturity. In a relational context, a resistant person loses trust in others because of their lack of willingness to resolve turmoil, most likely out of fear of being wrong or perceived as weak.

Linda was a hardworking manager at a software development firm. She had recently hired a new employee named Tom to work on a critical project. Tom had a lot of experience and seemed like a great addition to the team. Still, as soon as he started working, Linda noticed that he resisted taking direction from her.

Tom habitually did things his way and ignored Linda's suggestions. He was dismissive of her feedback and often rolled his eyes or argued with her when she tried to guide him. Linda found this behavior frustrating, but didn't want to start a conflict with Tom.

Linda noticed that Tom's resistance was causing delays and problems as the project progressed. He made decisions without consulting the rest of the team and often left critical tasks unfinished. This was starting to impact the project timeline, and Linda was worried that they wouldn't be able to deliver the product on time.

Linda tried to talk to Tom about his behavior, but he was dismissive and uncooperative. She tried to involve other team members in decision-making to keep things on track. Still, Tom's resistance made it difficult to get anything done. Eventually, the project fell behind schedule, and Linda was forced to report the delays to her superiors.

The ramifications of Tom's resistance were significant. The project missed its deadline, and the company lost a major client. Linda's team was demoralized, and morale throughout the company suffered. Linda's boss held her accountable and questioned her potential for future promotions.

In the end, Tom was let go from the company. He would become a resistant, know-it-all employee at the next company. The ramifications of Tom's resistant behavior had a lasting impact on Linda and the company, demonstrating the importance of being willing to work collaboratively.

A resistant person can create drama, and considerably damage team dynamics and organizations.

On the other hand, a responsive person responds quickly and appropriately to something that isn't right. This trait is one of the most critical ones for training children and a good quality for teammates. We want them to see when and where they are off and respond appropriately by making things right.

Need to or Want to (or Both)

Deciding whether to invest in a relationship is a highly personal decision that depends on various factors, including your values, goals, priorities, and relational dynamics. Family members are the most complicated decisions, as it is hard to fire a family member. It is much easier to pull back from someone who isn't a blood relative.

Here is a criteria filter to help you decide if you should lean in or out of a relationship:

1. Do you share similar values?
2. Is your communication open and healthy?
3. Are they willing to invest in you as much as you invest in them?
4. Is this the right time in your life to invest deeply in this relationship?
5. Is this person responsive or resistant?
6. Do you want to invest in a relationship or are you obliged to do so?

If this person is unwilling or able to invest in the relationship, it may not be worth pursuing.

Ultimately, the decision to invest in a relationship is a personal one that requires careful consideration and self-reflection.

It's essential to listen to your gut instincts and pay attention to any red flags or warning signs indicating the relationship is not a good fit. Trusting yourself and your instincts is vital to making the best decision and getting perspective from others you trust.

Relationships Are Worth It until They Aren't

A great relationship can bring a sense of fulfillment, joy, and purpose to your life. It can enhance your well-being and personal growth and provide you with a supportive and loving friend for life. Great relationships improve your mental health, bring emotional support, and enhance physical health.

Conversely, poor relationships bring emotional distress, decreased self-esteem, and cause stress that affects mental and physical health. It's essential to recognize the signs of a negative relationship and take steps to address them or end it if necessary. Professional help can be vital in overcoming the effects of a negative relationship.

> *"Relationships are worth fighting for, but you can't be the only one fighting."*—*Anonymous*

Amy worked in a small business in the central United States. Her colleague, Shane, had always been a helpful co-worker. They had worked together on several projects and had developed a good rapport. However, Shane became distant and unresponsive to Amy's emails and calls.

Amy was concerned about the change in Shane's behavior and tried to contact him to discuss the issue. However, Shane was dismissive and refused to engage in any meaningful conversation. Amy tried several times to get Shane to open up, but he remained evasive and unresponsive.

Despite her best efforts, Amy could not progress in repairing the relationship with Shane. She started to feel frustrated and disheartened by the lack of progress. She wondered what she could have done differently to change the outcome.

As time passed, Amy began to accept that repairing the relationship with Shane was impossible. She had tried everything she could think of, but Shane seemed uninterested in improving the relationship. The more she tried, the more complicated her life became. The stress began to affect other relationships until she reached the point where she chose to lean out and focus on other areas of her work and life.

While Amy was disappointed that she had not been able to restore the relationship with Shane, she took comfort in the fact that she had done everything she could to try to make it work. She realized that sometimes, some relationships cannot be salvaged no matter how hard you try. However, she also learned that it's essential to try to make things right and be willing to try to repair relationships, even if the outcome is not always what you hope for.

In the words of the immortal Will Rogers, "Never invest in a relationship where you have to buy a plot in the cemetery to keep it going."

Relationships are worth it until they aren't.

What Is the Cost of Not Working on It?

The relational cost of not addressing the historical relational dynamics and cracking someone's communication code is significant. Healthy communication is the foundation of any significant relationship. When one person's communication style or needs are not understood or acknowledged, it can lead to misunderstandings, hurt feelings, and ultimately, a damaged relationship.

For example, suppose someone tends to be indirect or use sarcasm to communicate, but their partner doesn't understand. In that case, it can lead to confusion and misinterpretation.

The partner may take offense or feel hurt by the sarcastic remarks, even though the other person didn't intend it that way. This can lead to resentment and misunderstandings, and ultimately, erode the trust and intimacy in the relationship.

Likewise, suppose someone has specific communication needs, such as needing time alone to process their thoughts or requiring explicit instructions, and their partner doesn't acknowledge or respect these needs. In that case, it can lead to frustration and conflict. The partner may feel their needs are unmet, leading to resentment and a communication breakdown.

The relational cost of not unlocking someone's Communication Code can be significant. It can lead to misunderstandings, hurt feelings, and ultimately, damage the relationship.

If you want to avoid this, understanding and acknowledging each other's communication styles and needs is essential. Understanding and truly listening to them can help to strengthen the relationship, build trust, and deepen intimacy.

Choosing to Lean Out

Choosing not to invest and engage in healthy communication with another person can have several adverse effects on them. Some of these effects may include:

1. Frustration and confusion: When you don't communicate effectively, the other person may become frustrated and

confused, especially if they are trying to understand your perspective or resolve an issue.

2. Resentment: If you are not willing to engage in healthy communication, the other person may feel resentful toward you. They may feel you are unwilling to listen or try to understand their point of view.
3. Lack of trust: When communication breaks down, it can lead to a lack of confidence in the relationship. The other person may begin to question your intentions or wonder if you are keeping things from them.
4. Emotionally drained: When healthy communication does not occur, the other person may become emotionally drained. They may feel like they are constantly walking on eggshells, or trying to guess your thoughts or feelings.
5. Relationship breakdown: If healthy communication is not taking place, it can lead to a breakdown in the relationship. The other person may feel like they cannot connect with you or that the relationship is not worth pursuing.

The choice is yours whether you lean in or out. Therefore, it's essential to communicate effectively and engage in healthy communication with the people in our lives.

Choosing to Lean In

When someone chooses to lean in and solve someone else's Communication Code, they can become more influential, which:

1. Builds trust: Taking the time and effort to understand someone's communication style and needs can help build trust between the two parties. The other person will feel

like their needs are being heard and respected, which can help to deepen the relationship and create a stronger bond.

2. Increases empathy: When someone takes the time to understand someone's Communication Code, it can increase their compassion for the other person. They will be better able to put themselves in the other person's shoes and see things from their perspective, leading to better communication and a deeper understanding of each other.
3. Facilitates problem solving: By understanding someone's communication code, it can help to facilitate problem solving. The two parties will be better able to communicate their needs and concerns, leading to more effective problem solving and resolution of issues.
4. Builds rapport: When someone takes the time to understand someone's Communication Code, it can help to build rapport between the two parties. They will feel more connected and aligned, leading to a more positive and productive relationship.

By leaning in and solving someone else's Communication Code, someone can become more influential by building trust, increasing empathy, facilitating problem solving, and building rapport. This can lead to a more substantial, positive, and productive relationship, benefiting both parties.

Regarding relationships, taking time and ensuring that investment makes sense is okay. Investing in the wrong person can waste time and energy, but investing in the right one can bring great rewards.

Will you experience fulfillment and support in a relationship if you invest 80% of your time and energy in the relationships that bring you the most joy, fulfillment, and support, and 20% in those that require more work or attention?

The Price:

The price of a relationship is the time, energy, and risk that come with investing in another person.

Henry David Thoreau aptly said, "The price of anything is the amount of life you exchange for it."

Based on all the preceding thoughts, is the exchange of a relationship worth the price?

The Prize:

The prize for a healthy relationship is immeasurable. There are joys from the companionship that are significant.

As the author Richard Rohr says, "The greatest joys and challenges of life come from relationships."

Relationships are complicated, and yet, worth it. They require balance and constant attention.

In the next chapter, we will go even deeper to look at how to salvage relationships that are not heading in the direction you want them to go.

11 Re-Establishing Communication

> *"We cannot solve our problems with the same thinking we used when we created them."*
> —Albert Einstein

The prefix *re-* is an essential piece of the idea of *re*-establishing communication. *Re-* means to back up and do something again. It means you get a second, third, or fourth chance to do something. *Re-* is a redo.

Re- can happen in

- resetting a relationship
- renewing a friendship
- repenting for past wrongs
- reviewing ways to improve
- rekindling a marriage, and so on

If you want to re-establish communication, and for that matter, an actual relationship, then it might be helpful to ponder these questions:

1. Where does *re-* need to take place?
2. What needs to be healed in the relationship?
3. What specifically needs to be renewed?

Luke and Allison had been married for 10 years. They had two children and a comfortable life. They were happy in many ways, but there was a growing distance between them. They had stopped communicating as they used to do when they were dating. They didn't laugh as much, and they didn't talk about their dreams and hopes. They were polite with each other, but it felt like they were strangers living in the same house.

Luke was a successful businessman who had always been ambitious and driven. He worked long hours and brought work home. He had little time for anything else, including his wife and children. Allison was a kind-hearted woman who had always supported her husband's career. But she had grown tired of feeling neglected and taken for granted.

One day, Allison finally had enough. She sat down with Luke and told him how she felt. Allison explained that she felt like she was living with a stranger and missed the man she had fallen in love with. She told him she needed him to listen to her and be there for her and their children. Luke was taken aback. He had no idea that his wife felt this way. He had always thought that providing for his family was enough.

Luke realized that his overworking was harming his wife. He was so focused on his career that he had forgotten to nurture his marriage. Luke knew that he needed to change and ask for forgiveness, but he didn't realize that her communication code had become more complex because of his absence. While she had tried to connect with him, he wasn't responsive, which caused her to pull back.

After a particularly hard conversation, Luke sat with Allison and apologized for his behavior. He told her that he was sorry for neglecting her and their family. He promised that he would do better and make more time for them. But he also realized that asking for forgiveness was not enough. He had to change himself before expecting Allison to see him differently.

Together, they met with a marriage counselor to improve their relationship. Luke stopped trying to solve her problems and instead asked her how he could help. He showed her he cared by paying attention to her needs and wants. He took the time to understand her, and in doing so, he unlocked her communication code.

Luke consciously tried to be more present in his family's life. He started to leave work and focus on his family when he was home. Luke asked Allison about her day and listened to her answers. He took an interest in their children's activities and spent more time with them.

Over time, Luke and Allison's relationship began to heal. They started to laugh together again, and talk about their dreams and hopes. They began to feel like a team again, working together to create a happy life. Luke had learned that communication is a two-way street and there was a code that could be used to connect more effectively.

Re-establishing good communication between two people requires effort and a willingness to change. Both parties must be committed to improving the situation and be open to feedback and new ideas.

> *"I have learned that sometimes 'sorry' is not enough. Sometimes you have to actually change."*
> *—Claire London*

In this chapter, you will learn how to re-establish communication if communication is broken.

Overcoming Relational Blockage

"Okay, I get it, guys," you say. "You just don't understand my family! The Communication Code won't work because we are too far gone—there is too much pain from the past."

"I just can't be around him. I lose my breath and can't think because of the pain he causes me." We have often heard this as one person explains their interaction with another person in their family.

We get it—we do. Some relationships have too much plaque built up from years of frustration or abuse that no amount of positive communication can change.

Relationships tend to go through stages. The scientific stages of relationships are a widely recognized concept in social psychology.

1. Acquaintanceship: This is the first stage of a relationship, where you meet someone and start to get to know them. You may share some common interests or activities, but have yet to learn from each other very well.
2. Buildup: In this stage, you develop a stronger connection with your friend. You may start spending more time together and sharing more personal information about yourselves.
3. Continuation: This stage involves maintaining your friendship over time. You may continue to share experiences and activities and provide emotional support for each other.
4. Deterioration: This stage involves a decline in the friendship, which may occur for various reasons, such as a change in interests or a lack of communication, or someone moving. You may find that you start to see your friend less frequently or that your interactions become less meaningful.
5. Repair: This stage involves working to repair any damage to the friendship. You may need to communicate with your friend to address any issues or misunderstandings that have arisen. Doing this well can lead to a renewal of the friendship. If not done well, it can lead to more deterioration or termination.
6. Termination: This is the final stage, where the friendship ends. This may happen naturally as you grow apart or result from a conflict or disagreement that cannot be resolved.

Any relational plaque from power plays or past hurts constricts communication and leads to relational blockage.

Remember, relational plaque buildup is the historical frustrations that come from domination, abdication, and long-term communication abuse, or it could be caused by different personalities that don't have the tools to connect once things become difficult. Relational plaque is similar to the physical plaque that enters hearts and reduces blood flow.

It's important to remember that friendships, like all relationships, require effort and communication to be successful. Not all friendships follow a linear path; some may skip certain stages or cycle through them multiple times. Being authentic, supportive, and understanding is the key to building lasting friendships.

Real-Life Scenarios

Many negative scenarios can arise in relationships when communication starts to break down and the relationship needs to be re-established. When communication starts to break down in a relationship, you will often see the following:

1. Misunderstanding and miscommunication
2. Negative emotions and behaviors
3. Disrespect and lack of trust
4. Power struggles and control issues
5. Betrayal/looking elsewhere to meet communication needs
6. Avoidance and withdrawal.

One of the most significant issues with communication breakdowns is that every human needs to connect, be heard, and be valued. When that does not come from those closest to us, we start to look to get those needs met elsewhere. We become resigned that things will not change in our current relationship; we've tried everything we know. We then find someone else who gets us, is easy to communicate with, and then we start to invest here. People are unfaithful in their communication long before they become unfaithful physically. It's a vicious cycle that takes intervention and help to repair.

If issues are not addressed, then people will become cold and distant.

Cold Heart Syndrome

"Cold heart" is a phrase that is often used in a figurative sense to describe someone who is emotionally distant, unfeeling, or lacks empathy. It can refer to a person who is cold or unresponsive in their interactions with others or is perceived as being indifferent to the feelings of others.

Re-establishing communication with someone who is cold and has their walls up requires patience, empathy, and a willingness to work toward a solution together. By showing that you are committed to improving the relationship, and willing to listen and work through any issues, you can gradually rebuild trust and strengthen your connection.

Just as the heart needs good blood flow to stay healthy and robust, relationships require good communication to thrive and succeed.

10 Ideas for Re-Establishing Communication

If both parties are prepared to deal with the past, and despite hesitations and fears, are prepared to try one last time, then here are some proven ideas that can help re-establish communication. We recommend working through this list together with a coach to help you process it effectively.

1. Walk in Their Shoes

To "walk in someone else's shoes" means to try to understand and empathize with another person's experiences, emotions, and perspectives by imagining yourself in their situation. It involves temporarily adopting their point of view to gain a deeper understanding of their thoughts, feelings, challenges, and motivations.

By metaphorically putting yourself in someone else's shoes, you attempt to see the world through their eyes and to experience what they might be going through. This practice helps foster empathy, compassion, and a broader perspective, allowing you to relate to others on a deeper level.

"Walk in someone else's shoes" encourages stepping outside of your own limited viewpoint and biases to consider different circumstances, backgrounds, and realities. It promotes understanding, tolerance, and the ability to make more informed judgments and decisions by considering multiple perspectives.

This idea serves as a reminder to approach others with empathy, to be mindful of their experiences, and to seek a deeper understanding of their lives before forming opinions or passing judgment.

Remember that rebuilding trust and communication takes time and may not happen overnight. Be patient and persistent, and continue to show that you are committed to improving the relationship.

2. Write the Letter

One exercise you can do to re-establish good communication with someone else is to write a letter expressing your thoughts and feelings.

Writing a letter can help you organize your thoughts and emotions and provide a clear and concise message to the other person.

In the letter, explain what happened, how you feel about it, and what you would like to happen moving forward. It is important to avoid blaming or attacking language and focus on using "I" statements to express your feelings and needs.

We encourage you not to share the letter, but to use the letter as a way to organize your thoughts and guide your conversation.

3. Practice Forgiveness

Forgiveness gives the relationship a chance to live again—it gives it a second chance. Resentment slams the door on any *re-* word working.

Do you need to forgive someone?

> *"Forgiveness does not change the past, but it does enlarge the future."—Paul Boese*

Do you need to ask for forgiveness from someone?

Jared and Amanda had been married for five years and were always very happy together. However, Amanda had become increasingly critical of Jared's behavior over the past year. She would criticize him for not doing the dishes, leaving his clothes lying around, or forgetting to take out the trash, thinking it was constructive critique.

At first, Jared tried to ignore Amanda's criticism, but it started to wear him down as time passed. He began to feel like he could never do anything right and started withdrawing from Amanda emotionally.

One day, after a particularly harsh critique, Jared sat down with Amanda and told her how he felt. He explained that his job was difficult, he needed to know she cared about him, and her criticism hurt him and made him feel like a failure as a husband.

At first, Amanda was defensive, insisting that she was only trying to help him be a better husband. But as Jared continued to share his feelings, she began to understand her words' impact on him.

Amanda apologized for her behavior and promised to try to be more supportive and to learn to offer care and maybe even some celebration as she became better with the communication code. Jared, in turn, decided to forgive her and work on rebuilding their relationship.

Over time, Jared and Amanda were able to repair their relationship and build a stronger foundation of trust and respect. Jared learned the power of forgiveness and realized that holding on to anger and resentment only hurt him in the long run. In forgiving Amanda, he could let go of his hurt and move forward with their relationship.

> *"To forgive is to set a prisoner free and discover that the prisoner was you."—Lewis B. Smedes*

What about you? Is it time to forgive someone for something?

4. Renew Your Vision

Vision is what you want in something or someone. It is a destination of what you hope for in the future. Every relationship has a vision that has been covered up or not met.

Renewing your vision can help re-establish communication with someone by providing clarity and direction for your actions and intentions. When you have a clear vision of what you want to achieve in a relationship, you can communicate more effectively and authentically with the other person.

By sharing your vision, you can express your values, hopes, and expectations in an inspiring and motivating way for both of you. You can also listen more attentively to the other person's vision and understand their perspective better. This creates a sense of shared purpose and commitment, which helps repair any damage to the relationship and build a stronger and more fulfilling connection.

5. Reset Expectations

With vision comes expectations, which is a version of hope. Expectations are your hopes organized. We discussed this in depth in Chapter 2.

Do you need to reset your expectations with a specific person?

Mahatma Gandhi was a powerful example of resetting expectations with his son.

Gandhi was known for his philosophy of nonviolent resistance and his work to free India from British rule. However, he also had a strained relationship with his son, Harilal.

Harilal struggled with alcoholism and refused to follow his father's teachings. Gandhi was disappointed in his son, and the two had a tumultuous relationship for many years.

However, toward the end of his life, Gandhi began to reevaluate his relationship with his son. He recognized that his expectations of Harilal may have been too high and needed to show him more love and understanding.

Gandhi wrote to Harilal, asking for forgiveness for any mistakes he had made as a father. He also expressed his hope that they could reconcile and rebuild their relationship.

Although the two never fully reconciled, this moment of reflection and renewed vision allowed Gandhi to make peace with his past and try to repair the damage in his relationship with his son.

We are not "Pollyanna" in all relationships. We realize that every relationship can't be solved or fixed, but as the Apostle Paul shares in the Bible in Romans 12:18, "If it is possible, as far as it depends on you, live at peace with everyone."

6. Re-Establish Communication Rhythm

Sometimes the best thing you can do in a relationship is reset when, where, and how you meet. Place and space can often hold memories in them.

Have you ever heard, "See that booth over there? That is where I asked your mother out on our first date," or "I don't want to go to that restaurant—there are too many bad memories there."

To do this well, you may have to change the following:

- Where to meet: Create new meeting points that don't carry with them any baggage or past negative energy.
- When you meet or connect: As life changes, it is helpful to find the best places that allow you both to connect without distraction.
- How you communicate: Video or face-to-face communication is always more effective. Be careful of text, DMs, or emails as your primary communication tool because so much of that communication can become misinterpreted.

7. *Manage Distractions*

One more important step in re-establishing communication is managing your distractions. Why? Because in a reset, people are hyper-focused on the minor things, and if they feel that you are not interested or that something is more important than that moment, they might exaggerate the situation and think, "This is useless. He will never change."

Don't give a chance for any plaque to resurface. Instead, manage your distractions.

Managing distractions can be challenging, but there are several strategies you can use to help stay focused and minimize interruptions. The following story provides some tips on how to manage distractions.

DJ and Joe had been friends for years, but their relationship had hit a rough patch recently. They decided to meet to discuss things and hopefully re-establish their friendship.

They met at a local coffee shop and sat down to talk. DJ was eager to listen and work things out, but Joe seemed distracted. He kept checking his phone, responding to texts, and scrolling through social media.

DJ tried to keep the conversation going, but Joe's lack of focus made it difficult. Finally, after Joe checked his phone for the third time in five minutes, DJ spoke up.

"Joe, I want to make this work, but it's hard when you're constantly checking your phone. Can we put them away for a little bit and focus on talking?"

Joe looked up, completely surprised. He said, "I think you are overreacting, DJ!" Joe was clueless that his action reminded Joe of the relational plaque that was built up.

Joe pulled back, and they ended their time with Joe being clueless and DJ deciding that this was not a relationship to invest in for the future.

This unawareness happens all the time. To re-establish anything, a person must be willing to focus on the other person without distraction.

8. Use the Communication Code

We have successfully used the Communication Code in everyday situations in various relationships. It works. We have thousands of stories and examples of how it has saved people from relational drama and reset communication in a way that leads to relational trust.

Practice it. Teach it, and eventually perfect it. If you need to review how to use it again, go to Chapter 3.

"Hey, Tom, let me clarify. Are you saying this?" Or, "Are you open to my collaboration on that?"

If someone uses the wrong Communication Code or isn't truly listening, believe the best and start the process again.

9. Try Love

One of the greatest quotes ever written comes from the Apostle Paul, "And now these three remain: faith, hope, and love. But the greatest of these is love."

We believe that love is fighting for the highest possible good of the other person. When they know you are for them and feel it consistently, they will be more prone to open up to you and allow you to influence them.

Try fighting for the highest good in them. That could include:

- Caring about the things they care about
- Learning to celebrate with them even if you are not a "celebrator"

- Listening far longer than you usually do
- Clarifying what they are saying versus assuming you know
- Asking them if you can collaborate or critique when appropriate

10. Establish Psychological Safety

To re-establish communication, you must provide psychological safety in the relationship. This means you help them feel comfortable and safe enough to express their thoughts, feelings, and ideas without fear of judgment, criticism, or adverse consequences.

It requires you to create a space of trust, respect, and openness where the other person can be vulnerable and take risks without worrying about rejection or punishment.

Psychological safety is crucial for rebuilding relationships and effective communication as it enables the other person to begin to trust you again. To do that well, consider the following list:

Relationships are worth fighting for—we need them to thrive as humans. "So far as it depends on you" is an excellent concept for re-establishing communication.

"True friendship comes when the silence between two people is comfortable." —David Tyson

The next chapter is designed to help you summarize everything you have learned in this book. Applied learning is the best learning. Don't miss the opportunity to create a plan that could quite possibly change a relationship for the better forever.

12 Your Communication Plan

"Communication works for those who work at it."
—John Powell

You made it! You have experienced our thoughts on relational dynamics and the code words needed to unlock the relationships in your life. You have gone through the gauntlet of understanding the stages of communication, and that communication is a two-way street (see Figure 12.1).

Effective communication requires understanding and attention to each of these stages. By being mindful of the message, channel, receiver, feedback, noise, and context, you can improve your communication skills and build stronger relationships with others.

It's now time to get practical. Think of two relationships (one from work and one at home) that you want to work on to improve. We are going to help you create your communication plan.

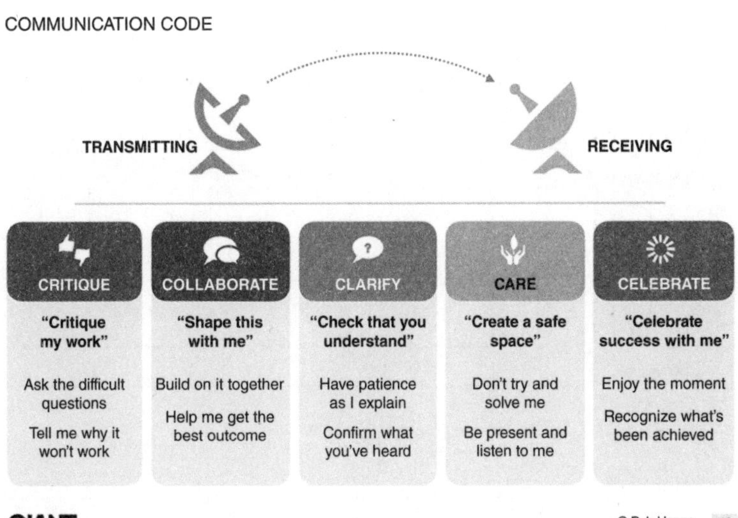

Figure 12.1 The Communication Code.

Who

Who are the people that you want to unlock a relationship?

Person 1: ______________________________

Person 2: ______________________________

What

What do you want to rebuild or hope happens with each?

Person 1: ______________________________

Person 2: ______________________________

What are your expectations for these people, and are they realistic?

Person 1: ______________________________

Person 2: ______________________________

What is the incentive for you to reestablish communication with each?

Person 1: ______________________________

Person 2: ______________________________

What is the Communication Code for each person?

Person 1: ______________________________

Person 2: ______________________________

Why

Why do you want to improve your relationship with them?

Person 1: ______________________________

Person 2: ______________________________

Why is it worth your time?

Person 1: ______________________________

Person 2: ______________________________

How

How do you plan to improve your relationships with them?

Person 1: ______________________________

Person 2: ______________________________

What specific strategies are you going to use for each to improve your communication?

Person 1: ______________________________

Person 2: ______________________________

When

When will you meet with them?

Person 1: ______________________________

Person 2: ______________________________

Where

Where will you meet to have a conversation?

Person 1: ______________________________

Person 2: ______________________________

We wish you the best as you journey to revolutionize every relationship. If you work at building healthy relationships, your opportunities for breakthrough will occur on a more regular basis.

Prevention

Remember these realities as you work to rebuild these relationships and leverage the communication code.

1. Remember the power of your presence: Your past will affect the present. As you get ready to meet with them to

strengthen, rebuild, or re-establish communication, think about what it is like on the other side of you.

Are you a strong personality, or is your presence ominous? Do what you must to create psychological safety to make your communication effective.

2. Practice support before challenge: If you are not showing up as a liberating person full of High support and High challenge, it won't be easy to reestablish anything. You must show people that you are for them, not just say it for their trust levels to increase with you.
3. Consistency is key: When people see you as reliable and stable over time, they will begin to lower their walls of self-preservation and let you into more of their lives. You must be predictable with your actions for relationships to improve.

Healthy communication is an exception, not the norm. However, if you decide to improve your communication intentionally, and thus, your relationship with another person, the odds are in your favor that you will have a breakthrough.

Committing to sending and receiving clear messages and developing healthy relationships is a mature goal of every person. We hope that you use the cipher and the tools we have provided to fight for the highest possible good in others and change the trajectory of the relationships in your life.

Make every conversation count. Understand the Communication Code of others and commit to using the cipher to unlock every relationship, one conversation at a time. By doing the hard work you just my find that you are starting to enjoy who you are becoming as you learn to enjoy who others are as well.

About the Authors

Jeremie Kubicek and Steve Cockram are co-founders of GiANT Worldwide, a content licensing software company specializing in leader and culture transformation in over 100 countries.

Along with *The Communication Code*, they have also written *The 5 Gears: How to Be Present and Productive When There Is Never Enough Time*; *The 5 Voices: How to Communicate Effectively with Everyone You Lead*; and *The 100X Leader: How to Become Someone Worth Following.* They are also co-creators of the premier GiANT Leadership Toolkit and share their experiences on the GiANT (Liberator) Podcast.

Jeremie Kubicek

Jeremie Kubicek is a *Wall Street Journal* bestselling author of *Making Your Leadership Come Alive*, *Leadership Is Dead*, *The Peace Index*, and co-author of the books listed in the preceding paragraph. He has been named consistently by *Inc.* magazine as a top-100 speaker and featured on MSNBC, *Inc.* magazine,

Entrepreneur, and inside many of the largest companies in the world.

Jeremie is a serial entrepreneur and is co-founder of GiANT, Six Summers (SixSummers.com), Zoey (Zoey.io), and Better (BeBetterLeaders.com), where he also provides sports performance expertise to the University of Oklahoma football team.

Jeremie and his family have lived in Moscow, Atlanta, London, and Oklahoma City. He and his wife, Kelly, have three grown children: Addison, Will, and Kate. They also run their Farmstead Venue (FarmsteadVenue.com) for retreats and events. Jeremie spends most of his time enjoying travels, creating content, and encouraging people.

Find out more at www.jeremiekubicek.com.

Steve Cockram

Steve Cockram is an inspirational communicator, serial entrepreneur, and confidante to elite leaders around the world. He shares practical, actionable wisdom captured in memorable visual tools he uses daily with his family, team, and private consulting clients. He is highly skilled at making people think, laugh, and take action. Steve is an engaging, self-deprecating storyteller who uses his disarming British humor to draw in his audiences.

Steve and his family have lived on the moors of Yorkshire, the desert in Arizona, Pawleys Island in South Carolina, the hills of Devon, and now in West London. He and his wife, Helen, have three daughters—Izzy, Megan, and Charlie. He has a long-standing addiction to Test Match Cricket, and Harewood Downs Golf Course is his spiritual home. He loves walking, watching movies, and eating long dinners with good friends.

Find out more at www.stevecockram.com.

Index